Scott Foresman - Addison Wesley
MATH

Practice Workbook

Grade 5

Scott Foresman - Addison Wesley

Editorial Offices: Menlo Park, California • Glenview, Illinois
Sales Offices: Reading, Massachusetts • Atlanta, Georgia • Glenview, Illinois
Carrollton, Texas • Menlo Park, California

http://www.sf.aw.com

Overview

The *Practice Workbook* provides additional practice on the concept or concepts taught in each core lesson.

For Learn and Explore lessons, the worksheets provide additional exercises that reflect those in the Connect section and/or the Skills and Reasoning section of the student edition Practice sets.

For Problem Solving lessons, the worksheets closely mirror the Problem Solving Practice exercises in the student edition.

The *Practice Workbook* also includes Section Reviews that supplement the Section Review pages in the student edition. These Section Review worksheets also provide Mixed Review problems (from previous sections of the student edition). Cumulative Review worksheets are included at the end of each chapter to provide a comprehensive review of skills covered up through that chapter.

ISBN 0-201-31246-8

Printed in the United States of America

14 15 16 17 18   VHG   06 05 04 03

Contents

Name _____

Reading Graphs

Use the bar graph to answer **1–5**.

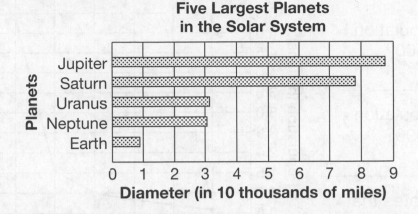

**Five Largest Planets
in the Solar System**

1. Which is the largest planet in the solar system? _____

2. Which planet has a diameter of about 80,000 miles? _____

3. About how many miles is Neptune's diameter? _____

4. Which planet is second largest? _____

5. About how much larger is Jupiter's diameter than Saturn's?

_____

Use the line plot to answer **6–11**.

**Count of Students'
Brothers and Sisters**

6. How many students have no brothers or sisters?

_____

7. How many students have 1 brother or sister?

_____

8. What is the most common number of brothers and sisters that students have? _____

9. How many classmates have more than 3 brothers and sisters? _____

10. How many students have less than 3 brothers and sisters? _____

11. How many students were questioned for this line plot? _____

Name _____

Reading Line Graphs

Use the line graph
to answer **1–11**.

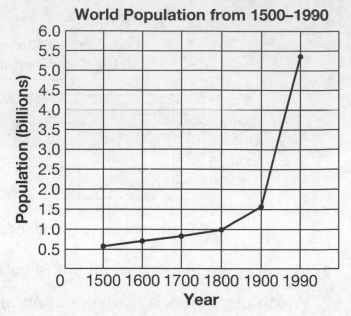

World Population from 1500–1990

1. What was the population
   of the world in 1500?

   _____

2. What was the population
   of the world in 1990?

   _____

3. Write the coordinates that
   represent the world
   population in 1600.

   _____

4. About how many more people
   were there in 1700 than in 1500? _____

5. What has happened to the
   world population since 1500? _____

6. Between which years was the
   increase in population the greatest? _____

   What was the increase? _____

7. Between which years was the
   increase in the population the least? _____

   What was the increase? _____

8. In which year was the population the least? _____

9. In which year was the population the greatest? _____

10. Write the coordinates that represent the
    number of people in 1800.

    _____

11. What is the scale on the horizontal axis?

    _____

Reading Stem-and-Leaf Plots

Every year, the best soccer teams in the state play in
a state tournament. This plot shows the number of
times the top nine teams have played in this tournament.

Use the plot to answer **1–4**.

Stem	Leaf
2	6 4 1
1	4 0
0	8 6 6 5

1. In what order are the stems arranged from top to bottom?

_____

2. How many teams have played 20 times or more? _____

3. Middletown has played in the state tournament the
second greatest number of times. How many times have
they played?

_____

4. River City and Yorktown have each played in the
state tournament the same number of times. How
many times have they played in the tournament? _____

Mr. Morgan's class took part
in a read-a-thon. This plot
shows how many books his
students read.

Stem	Leaf
2	4 3 1 2 0
1	9 4 3 7 4 0 0
0	8 9 3 9 9 8 5

Use the plot to answer **5-9**.

5. Emma read the most books. How many did she read? _____

6. How many students participated in the read-a-thon? _____

7. Did most students read more than 15 books? Explain.

_____

8. How many students read more than 20 books? _____

9. What was the least number of books read? _____

Range, Mode, and Median

This line plot shows the number of hours spent doing homework for a week.

Use the line and plot to answer **1** and **2**.

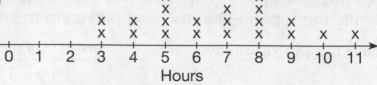

Hours Spent Doing Homework

Hours

1. For the above data, give the

   a. range _____   **b.** mode _____

   c. median _____

2. Did about half the students do homework for less than 6 hours?

   Explain. _____

   _____

Use the stem-and-leaf plot to answer **3–4**.

3. Give the: **a.** range _____

   b. mode _____

   c. median _____

4. Did the Dallas Cowboys score more than 26 points in about half of the games they played in 1995? Explain.

Points Scored by the Dallas Cowboys
(1995)

Stem	Leaf
3	5 1 4 4 4 4 7
2	3 3 3 8 0 4 1
1	7 7

_____

Use the line plot to answer **5–6**.   **Price of Inline Skates**

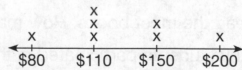

5. Give the:

   a. range _____   **b.** mode _____   **c.** median _____

6. Is it true that most of the inline skates cost less than $100? Explain.

_____

Introduction to the Problem Solving Guide

How many BMX and mountain bikes were sold?

You can use the bar graph to learn how many BMX and mountain bikes were sold.

Use the graph to answer **1–5**.

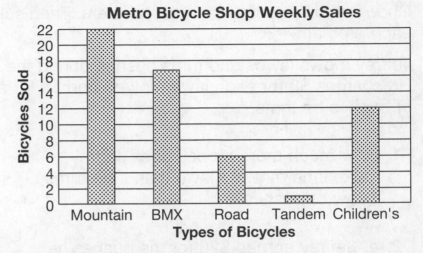

1. What information do you need to answer the question?

_____

2. What operation would you use to solve the problem? _____

3. Give the answer. _____

Choose the number sentence you would use to solve the problem.

4. How many more mountain bikes were sold than road bikes? _____

    A. 22 + 6 = 28   **B.** 22 – 6 = 16

5. What is the total number of road and tandem bikes sold? _____

    A. 6 + 1 = 7   **B.** 6 – 1 = 5

Use any strategy to solve each problem.

6. Roger bought a mountain bike for $130. He used $85 of his own money, and his father paid the rest. How much did his father pay? _____

7. One family bought 3 children's bicycles. Each cost the same amount. If their total bill was $225, what was the cost of each bicycle? _____

8. For 4 days, the bicycle shop sold the same number of bicycles each day. They sold a total of 52 bicycles in all. How many did they sell on the first day? _____

Analyze Word Problems: Choose an Operation

Choose the operation for each problem. Then solve each problem.

Jeffrey mows lawns and trims bushes during the spring. He charges $8 for each lawn mowed and $4 for each row of bushes he trims.

1. How much more money does Jeffrey make if he mows 1 lawn than if he trims 1 row of bushes?

_____

2. a. Jeffrey earned $20 for the bushes he trimmed. How many rows of bushes did he trim?

_____

b. How much money did he make mowing 5 lawns?

_____

c. How much did he earn in all?

_____

Write the operation needed for each problem. Then solve each problem.

3. Martina delivers newspapers to 60 houses on her route. She had so many customers, she decided to give 12 customers to her brother. To how many houses does Martina deliver now?

_____

4. Louisa charges each customer the same amount to rake leaves. In one week, 3 of her customers paid her $18.75. How much did each customer pay?

_____

5. Steven drinks 3 glasses of water a day. How many glasses of water does he drink in a week?

_____

Exploring Algebra: What's the Rule?

Find the rule for each table. Give the rule using words and a variable.

1.

A	B
3	1
9	3
12	4
18	6
21	7

_____

_____

2.

A	B
0	0
14	2
28	4
35	5
49	7

_____

_____

3.

A	B
1	6
7	12
11	16
15	20
21	26

_____

_____

Complete each table. Give its rule using words and a variable.

4.

A	B
☐	18
9	27
12	☐
15	45
18	54

5.

A	B
8	1
48	☐
56	7
☐	8
72	9

6.

_____

_____

Write each rule using a variable.

7. Divide a number by 8

_____

8. 2.1 more than a number

_____

Write each rule using words.

9. $n \times 12$

_____

10. $n \div 6$

_____

Name _____

Review and Practice

(Lesson 1) Use the line plot to answer **1** and **2**.

Scores Earned on Test

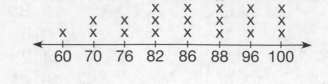

1. How many students earned less

   than 80 on the test? _____

2. What score was earned by the greatest number of students? _____

(Lesson 2) Use the line graph to answer **3–5**.

Distance Traveled

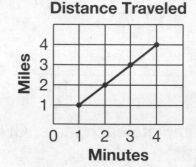

3. What does this line graph show? _____

   _____

   _____

4. What distance was traveled in 4 minutes? _____

5. What does the ordered pair (3,3) stand for?

   _____

(Lessons 3 and 4) Use this stem-and-leaf plot to answer **6–8**.

Stem	Leaf
0	7 8 9 9 9
1	3 3 4 6
2	1 1 2 3 4
3	0 1

6. What is the mode for the number of pages read? _____

7. What is the range of the number of pages read? _____

8. What is the median number of pages read? _____

(Lessons 5 and 6) Solve.

9. The average number of books Jill reads per month is 4. About how many books will she read in 6 months? _____

(Lesson 7) Complete the table. Write its rule using a variable.

10.

A	1	3	5	7	9
B	5	15	___	___	___

Rule: _____

(Mixed Review) Find each sum or difference.

11. $16 + 9 =$ _____   12. $24 - 8 =$ _____

13. $17 - 9 =$ _____   14. $6 + 36 =$ _____

Scales and Bar Graphs

Use the graphs to answer 1–5.

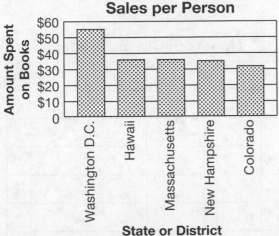

**Graph A
Average Annual Book
Sales per Person**

Amount Spent on Books

$60 $50 $40 $30 $20 $10 0

Washington D.C. | Hawaii | Massachusetts | New Hampshire | Colorado

State or District

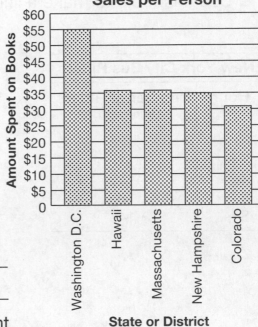

**Graph B
Average Annual Book
Sales per Person**

Amount Spent on Books

$60 $55 $50 $45 $40 $35 $30 $25 $20 $15 $10 $5 0

Washington D.C. | Hawaii | Massachusetts | New Hampshire | Colorado

State or District

1. What is the scale of Graph A? _____

2. What is the scale of Graph B? _____

3. Do both graphs show the same amount
   of money spent on books in each state? _____

4. Which graph implies the least difference in the
   amount of money spent on books in each state? _____

5. Which graph is easier to read? Explain. _____

_____

6. Choose a scale and make a bar
   graph of the data in the table.

Patton Middle School Students' Favorite Colors	
Color	**Number of Students**
blue	14
red	29
hot pink	25
green	12
yellow	36

7. What scale did you choose? Why?

_____

_____

Exploring Making Line Graphs

1. Line graphs are used to show changes

or _____ in data.

2. Use this table to make a line graph.

New York City Bus Riders	
Hour	**Number of Riders** (thousands)
12 P.M.	125
2 P.M.	115
4 P.M.	140
6 P.M.	185
8 P.M.	145

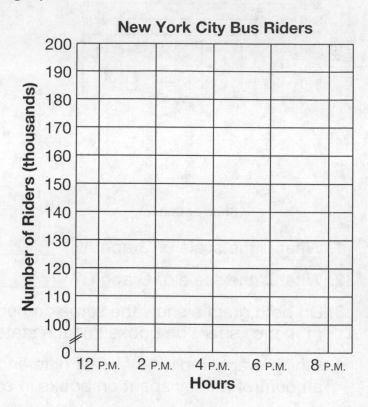

3. Use the graph to determine about how many riders there

would be at 3 P.M. _____

_____

4. a. Between which times shown on the graph did the number

of riders decrease? _____

_____

b. Why do you think fewer people traveled at these times?

_____

_____

Exploring Making Stem-and-Leaf Plots

1. Make a stem-and-leaf plot for the temperature data.

Daily Highs for the Month of July
in degrees Farenheit
88 74 78 86 90 91 94 92 85 87 83 79
81 90 87 84 83 79 84 85 90 83 78 83

Stem	Leaf

2. Most of the temperatures fell between _____ and _____ degrees.

Use the table to answer **3–8**.

National Ice Hockey Final 1995–1996 Standings			
Atlantic Division	**Wins**	**Pacific Division**	**Wins**
Washington	39	Colorado	47
New Jersey	37	Vancouver	32
Philadelphia	45	Anaheim	35
New York	22	Calgary	34
Tampa Bay	38	Los Angeles	24
Florida	41	Edmonton	30
New York	41	San Jose	20

3. Make a stem-and-leaf plot for the Atlantic Division wins.

Stem	Leaf

4. Make a stem-and-leaf plot for the Pacific Division wins.

Stem	Leaf

5. Which division had more teams win 40–49 games?

_____

6. Which division had only one team win less than 30 games?

_____

7. The median number of games won by the:

Atlantic Division: _____   Pacific Division: _____.

8. Describe the shapes of stem–and–leaf plots for the divisions.

_____

_____

Analyze Strategies: Use Logical Reasoning

Use logical reasoning to solve each problem.

1. A family of four—mother, father, son, and daughter—sits down to have dinner together. Father and son sit across from one another, while the daughter sits to her father's right. Where does each person sit?

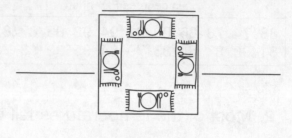

2. At a fast food restaurant, Peter and Patricia can choose from burgers, hot dogs, chicken, and fish. Peter and Patricia both eat two entrees, but neither eats the same one. Patricia is allergic to fish. Neither Peter nor Patricia will eat a burger and chicken together. What entrees did each choose?

_____

_____

_____

Use any strategy to solve each problem.

3. Here is some information about campers' favorite card games. No one liked to play *Old Maid*. *Go Fish* was liked slightly better than *Snap*, but not as well liked as *500 Rummy*. *War* got one more vote than *Old Maid*. *Concentration* was more favored than *Go Fish*, but just a little less liked than *500 Rummy*. List the order of the campers' favorite games.

_____

4. A road cleanup crew needs 2 volunteers for every 15 miles of road. If there are 60 miles of roads to be cleaned, how many volunteers are needed? _____

5. A cook wants to use $150 to buy hams and turkeys. The hams cost $45 and turkeys cost $35. How many hams and turkeys can the cook buy?

_____

Review and Practice

(Lesson 8) Choose a scale and make a bar graph of the data in the table.

1.

Technology in the Home	
Technology	**Number of Students**
Television	25
Telephone	21
VCR	15
Computer	5

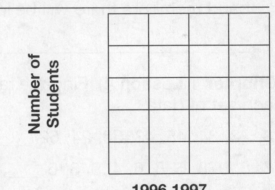

Technology

Number of Students

(Lesson 9) Make a line graph. Use the data in the table.

2.

Enrollment at East Elementary	
Year	**Number of Students**
1996	370
1997	375
1998	382

Number of Students

1996 1997

(Lesson 10) Make a stem-and-leaf plot for the data given.

3.

Height in Inches of Students in Mr. Young's Math Class
60 55 54 51 49 61 62 62 63
48 55 62 66 66 63 59 50

(Mixed Review) Find each product or quotient.

4. $5 \times 7 =$ _____   **5.** $56 \div 8 =$ _____   **6.** $7 \times 9 =$ _____

7. $32 \div 4 =$ _____   **8.** $25 \div 5 =$ _____   **9.** $6 \times 7 =$ _____

10. $18 \div 3 =$ _____   **11.** $4 \times 7 =$ _____   **12.** $81 \div 9 =$ _____

Cumulative Review

(Chapter 1 Lessons 2 and 9) Use the data to complete the line graph and answer the question.

1.

Number of Band Members per Year	
Year	**Number**
1995	40
1996	50
1997	55
1998	58

Number

0

Year

2. What can you predict about the number of band members there will be in the future?

_____

(Chapter 1 Lesson 4) Find the range, mode, and median for each set of data.

3. 23, 34, 45, 43, 56, 24, 62 _____, _____, _____

4. 8, 9, 8, 6, 8, 6, 4, 9, 3, 6 _____, _____, _____

(Chapter 1 Lesson 8) Use the data to complete the bar graph.

5.

Number of Instruments in the Band	
Instrument	**Number**
Clarinet	12
Flute	8
Trombone	4
Saxophone	3
Trumpet	10

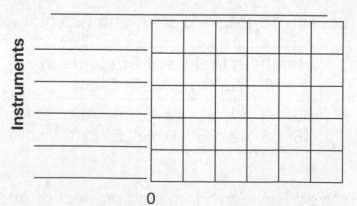

Instruments

0

Number

(Facts Review) Add, subtract, multiply or divide.

6. $2 \times 6 =$ _____   **7.** $45 \div 9 =$ _____   **8.** $3 \times 12 =$ _____

9. $4 + 7 =$ _____   **10.** $17 - 9 =$ _____   **11.** $15 + 8 =$ _____

Name _____

Exploring a Million

Use a calculator to answer **1–2**.

1 hour = 60 minutes   1 day = 24 hours   1 week = 7 days

1. If your heart beats 70 times every minute, how many times does it beat:

    a. in one hour? _____   **b.** in 3 hours? _____

    c. in one day? _____   **d.** in one week? _____

2. How long would it take for your heart to beat 1,000,000 times? _____

Use patterns to solve **3–7**.

3. Suppose you have sheets of grid paper that are 5 × 5. Would you need more or less of these sheets than the 10 × 10 sheets to show one million squares? Explain.

_____

_____

4. A roll of pennies holds 100 pennies. How many pennies are in:

    a. 3 rolls? _____

    b. 10 rolls? _____

    c. 100 rolls? _____

    d. 1,000 rolls? _____

5. How many rolls of pennies makes one million pennies? _____

6. 500 pennies are worth $5. How much are each of these groups of pennies worth in dollars?

    a. 800 pennies = $ _____   **b.** 1,000 pennies = $ _____

    c. 5,000 pennies = $ _____   **d.** 25,000 pennies = $ _____

7. How much is one million pennies worth in dollars? _____

Place Value Through Millions

Write each number in word form.

1. 2,430,156 _____

_____

2. 83,705,019 _____

_____

3. 614,720,308 _____

_____

Write each number in standard form.

4. fifty-three million, two hundred
sixteen thousand, eight hundred four _____

5. four hundred sixty-four million,
five hundred two thousand, forty-three _____

6. seven million, seventy-six
thousand, two hundred eighty-nine _____

7. 80,000,000 + 9,000,000 +
400,000 + 7,000 + 200 + 60 + 5 _____

8. 100,000,000 + 10,000,000 +
7,000,000 + 300,000 + 50,000 + 600 + 50 _____

9. Look at these numbers.

3,500   30,500   3,000,500

a. How are the three numbers alike? _____

_____

b. How are the three numbers different? _____

_____

_____

© Scott Foresman Addison Wesley 5

Exploring Place-Value Relationships

Complete the following pattern.

1. $100 = 10 \times$ _____ $= 10^{\square}$

2. $1,000 =$ _____ $\times$ _____ $\times$ _____ $= 10^{\square}$

3. $10,000 =$ _____ $= 10^{\square}$

4. $100,000 =$ _____ $=$ _____

5. $1,000,000 =$ _____ $=$ _____

6. How many 10s make 100? _____

7. How many 100s make 100,000? _____

8. How many 1,000s make 100,000? _____

9. How many 10,000s make 1 million? _____

10. How many 100s make 1 million? _____

Write each number using exponents.

11. 10,000 _____

12. 10 _____

13. 1,000 _____

14. 1,000,000 _____

15. 100,000 _____

16. 100 _____

Complete.

17. $10^{\square} = 10,000,000$ **18.** $10^{\square} = 100,000,000$

19. $\square^2 = 100$ **20.** $10^{\square} = 10,000$

21. How does the number on the right of the equals sign
help you to find the exponents in **17–20**?

_____

Place Value Through Billions

Write each number in standard form.

1. three billion, six hundred million,
thirty thousand

_____

2. seventy-eight billion, forty-two million,
nine thousand, eleven

_____

3. four hundred billion, ninety million

_____

4. thirty billion, three hundred million,
thirty thousand, three hundred three

_____

Complete.

5. 130,009,400,660 = one hundred thirty _____, _____

million, four _____ thousand, six hundred sixty

6. 42,100,080,005 = _____ billion,

one _____, eighty _____, five

7. 900,090,700,007 = nine _____, _____ million,

seven _____, seven

8. How many 1,000,000s in 1,000,000,000? _____

9. How many 1,000s in 1,000,000,000? _____

10. How many 100,000,000s in fifty billion? _____

Write the place-value position for each digit in 240,786,305,900.

11. 6 _____   **12.** 4 _____

13. 2 _____   **14.** 8 _____

15. 7 _____   **16.** 3 _____

17. In the number 7,472,352,101 give the value of each 7.

_____

Comparing and Ordering

Write >, <, or = to complete.

1. 94,276 ◯ 89,376   **2.** 14,050 ◯ 9,876

3. 472,343 ◯ 473,668   **4.** 2,202,020 ◯ 2,202,020

5. five hundred thirty-six thousand ◯ 537,719

6. 16,740,280 ◯ sixteen million, four hundred seventy thousand, two hundred, eighty

7. 30 billion, 20 thousand ◯ 89 million, 60 thousand

8. seven million, six hundred thousand, fifty ◯ 7,603,050

9. 419,786,372 ◯ four hundred nineteen billion, six

Order these numbers from least to greatest.

10. 421,089   376,005   377,500   420,980

_____

11. 78,400,000   78,004,000,000   78,000,004

_____

12. 54,798   54,978   54,897   53,999

_____

13. 911,345   910,435   901,435   911,453

_____

14. 28,079,043   28,709,043   28,719,043

_____

15. What digit could be in the ten millions place of a number that is greater than 25,000,000 but less than 73,000,000? Explain.

_____

_____

Name _____

Rounding Greater Numbers

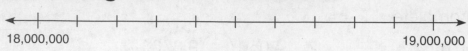

18,000,000   19,000,000

1. Use the number line to help you
round 18,521,425 to the nearest million. _____

Round to the nearest hundred thousand.

2. 872,768 _____   **3.** 8,243,956 _____

4. 2,035,467 _____   **5.** 43,974,012 _____

Round to the nearest million.

6. 8,643,231 _____   **7.** 75,499,999 _____

8. 987,645,312 _____   **9.** 489,753,274 _____

Round to the nearest ten million.

10. 78,634,021 _____   **11.** 7,630,998,432 _____

12. 646,000,000 _____   **13.** 801,009,999 _____

14. If 789,364,768 rounds to 789,400,000, to which place did you round?

_____

15. What is the greatest number that rounds to
65,000,000 when rounded to the million place? _____

Use the table to answer **16** and **17**.

16. Which city has a population
closest to 1,000,000 people?

_____

17. Which two cities would have
the same population if
rounded to the nearest 10,000?

City	Population in 1990
Austin, Texas	846,227
Louisville, Kentucky	948,829
Memphis, Tennessee	1,007,306
Las Vegas, Nevada	852,737

_____

Name _____

Review and Practice

Vocabulary Write whether each is true or false.

1. A period is one of the symbols: 0, 1, 2, 3, 4, 5, 6, 7, 8, 9. _____

2. A number line shows numbers in order. _____

3. A digit is a group of three numbers. _____

(Lesson 1) What is the value in dollars of the money in each stack?

4. one hundred $10 bills _____   **5.** ten $100 bills _____

(Lesson 3) Complete.

6. $10 \times$ _____ $= 50,000$ **7.** _____ $\times 800 = 80,000$

8. $10^{\square} = 100,000$

(Lessons 2 and 4) In the number 79,402,356,108 write the value of:

9. 4 _____   **10.** 7 _____

11. 9 _____   **12.** 2 _____

13. Write one hundred fifty million, two hundred fifty-seven thousand,

nine hundred forty-five in standard form. _____

(Lesson 5) Write >, <, or = to complete.

14. 235,641 $\bigcirc$ 93,584   **15.** 90,006 $\bigcirc$ ninety thousand six

16. 899,002 $\bigcirc$ six hundred million   **17.** 89,903 $\bigcirc$ 89,099

(Lesson 6) Use the table to answer **18** and **19**.

18. Write the letter for the breed
that has registered about:

   a. 70,000 dogs _____

   b. 100,000 dogs _____

19. To the nearest thousand, how
many Labrador retrievers are
registered? _____

Top 5 American Kennel Club Registrations	
Breed	**Registrations**
A. Labrador Retrievers	124,899
B. Rottweilers	104,160
C. German Shepherds	79,936
D. Cocker Spaniels	75,882
E. Golden Retrievers	68,125

(Mixed Review) Find each product or quotient.

20. $36 \div 9 =$ _____   **21.** $7 \times 7 =$ _____   **22.** $48 \div 6 =$ _____

Tenths and Hundredths

Write each decimal shown.

1. _____

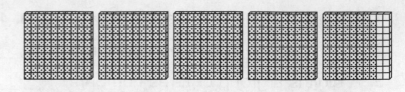

2. _____

Draw place-value blocks to show each decimal.

3. 0.56

4. 4.30

Write each number in decimal form.

5. 40 hundredths

6. 6 tenths

7. 4

_____

_____

_____

8. three and seventy-four hundredths _____

9. seven and three hundredths _____

10. Can you show 0.02 using only tenths place-value
blocks? Explain.

_____

_____

11. Which is greater, 5.34 or 5.43? Do you have to look at
the hundredths place to decide? Explain.

_____

Exploring Equivalent Decimals

Complete. Write =, >, or < for each answer.

1. 0.04 ◯ 0.40   **2.** 0.50 ◯ 0.5

3. 1.40 ◯ 14.0   **4.** 2.3 ◯ 2.30

Write two decimals that name each shaded part.

5. _____   **6.** _____

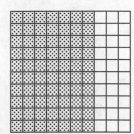   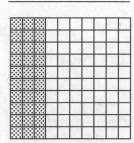

Write each as an equivalent decimal using tenths.

7. 0.20   **8.** 0.60   **9.** 0.80   **10.** 0.40

_____   _____   _____   _____

Write each as an equivalent decimal using hundredths.

11. 0.1   **12.** 0.6   **13.** 0.7   **14.** 0.3

_____   _____   _____   _____

In each group, write which decimals are equivalent.

15. 0.2 0.20 0.02   **16.** 0.40 0.04 0.4   **17.** 0.5 0.05 0.50

_____   _____   _____

18. On a hot summer's day, you read the temperature
on two different thermometers. The first
thermometer reads 90.9°F. The second
thermometer reads 90.90°F. Did you get the
same reading on both thermometers? Explain. _____

Thousandths

Write each number in decimal form.

1. 8 tenths _____

2. 8 hundredths _____

3. 800 thousandths _____

4. 8 thousandths _____

5. 8 _____

6. four and three tenths _____

7. eight and three hundredths _____

8. six and one tenth _____

9. four and sixty-six hundredths _____

10. three and eight thousandths _____

11. nine and six hundred eighty-eight thousandths _____

12. one and one hundred eleven thousandths _____

13. nine and twenty-one thousandths _____

14. two and one hundred nine thousandths _____

15. Which is greatest and which is least? 9.9, 9.09, 9.990? Explain.

_____

_____

_____

16. Using the digits 0, 4, 7, and 9, write the greatest decimal possible, in thousandths.

___ . ___ ___ ___

17. Using the digits 0, 3, 5, and 9, write the least decimal possible, in thousandths.

___ . ___ ___ ___

Decimals on the Number Line

Complete the number line.

1.
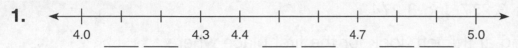

4.0   ____ ____   4.3   4.4   ____ ____   4.7   ____ ____   5.0

Name the number shown by each letter.

2.
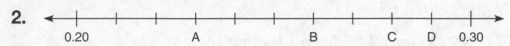

0.20   A   B   C   D   0.30

A _____   B _____   C _____   D _____

Use the number line shown to answer **3** and **4**. Name two numbers:

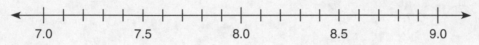

7.0   7.5   8.0   8.5   9.0

3. Between 7.5 and 8.0 _____

4. Between 8.0 and 8.5 _____

Use the number line shown to answer **5–7**.

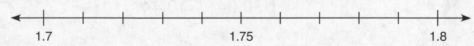

1.7   1.75   1.8

5. Name three numbers between 1.7 and 1.8. _____

_____

6. Is 1.799 between 1.7 and 1.8? Explain your thinking. _____

_____

7. Is 1.07 the half-way point between 1.7 and 1.8? Tell how you know.

_____

Name _____

Exploring Comparing and Ordering Decimals

1. Compare 3.277 and 3.274.

   a. Starting at the left, look for the first place where the digits are different. What place is it?

   _____

   b. Which number is greater? _____

2. Order 3.277, 3.274, and 3.27 from greatest to least by comparing numbers two at a time. Use > or < to compare.

   a. 3.277 ◯ 3.274

   b. 3.274 ◯ 3.27

   c. The order from greatest to least is _____

3. Order 0.4, 0.04, 4.00, and 0.44 from least to greatest by comparing numbers two at a time. Use < or > to compare.

   a. 0.04 ◯ 0.4   **b.** 0.04 ◯ 0.44

   c. 0.44 ◯ 4.00

   d. The order from least to greatest is _____

Write >, <, or = to complete.

4. 0.2 ◯ 0.03   **5.** 0.4 ◯ 0.54   **6.** 0.89 ◯ 2.1

7. 0.7 ◯ 79   **8.** 0.4 ◯ 0.44   **9.** 0.2 ◯ 0.20

10. 2.6 ◯ 2.36   **11.** 3.9 ◯ 3.09   **12.** 0.1 ◯ 0.16

13. 0.3 ◯ 0.34   **14.** 4.1 ◯ 4.19   **15.** 2.1 ◯ 2.10

16. 0.3 ◯ 0.03   **17.** 0.5 ◯ 0.56   **18.** 8.7 ◯ 8.07

19. 7.3 ◯ 7.33   **20.** 3.39 ◯ 33.9   **21.** 5.1 ◯ 5.09

Rounding Decimals

Round each number to the place of the underlined digit.

1. 7<u>3</u>.49

2. 2.<u>0</u>09

3. 36.4<u>1</u>5

4. <u>4</u>.708

_____

_____

_____

_____

5. 0.<u>8</u>2

6. 0.8<u>8</u>7

7. <u>9</u>.77

8. 2.<u>2</u>07

_____

_____

_____

_____

9. 7.7<u>5</u>7

10. 46.<u>9</u>60

11. 4<u>2</u>.59

12. <u>9</u>.65

_____

_____

_____

_____

13. 0.<u>6</u>8

14. 34.2<u>2</u>5

15. 4.<u>0</u>5

16. <u>4</u>.56

_____

_____

_____

_____

17. 19.<u>0</u>1

18. 0.08<u>7</u>

19. 4.0<u>5</u>0

20. <u>6</u>.957

_____

_____

_____

_____

21. <u>0</u>.3

22. 0.<u>8</u>24

23. <u>3</u>.989

24. 6.<u>0</u>64

_____

_____

_____

_____

25. 48.<u>0</u>5

26. <u>3</u>.25

27. 0.<u>8</u>57

28. 0.0<u>5</u>5

_____

_____

_____

_____

29. 7.0<u>1</u>9

30. 11.2<u>9</u>7

31. 3.<u>5</u>4

32. <u>0</u>.9

_____

_____

_____

_____

33. Name two decimals with digits in the hundredths place
that could be rounded to the tenths place as 0.4.

_____

_____

34. Name two decimals with digits in the tenths place that
could be rounded to the ones place as 1.

_____

_____

Analyze Strategies: Draw a Picture

Draw a picture to solve.

1. Jessica, Sarah, Annie, Tiffany, and Megan decide to go to an early movie that will cost them each $4. Jessica and Tiffany want to split a container of popcorn that costs $2. Megan and Annie want to share nachos that cost $4. Sarah wants to buy the souvenir movie poster for $3. Everyone brings $6.

   a. Will everyone have enough money for the movie and the items they want to buy?

   _____

   b. Who will spend the most money? _____

   c. How much money will Jessica have left? _____

2. Sam is 12 years old. Garrett is younger than Sam but older than David and Mark. David is 9 and Mark is 10.

   What is Garrett's age? _____

3. The school is having a skating party. The students decide to do a line dance. They form three lines. The longest line is 60 students. One of the other lines has half as many students but is twice as long as the third line. How many students are in each of the other two lines?

   _____

4. Danny, Philip, Jennifer, and Emily are having a bike race. Jennifer only finishes ahead of Philip, who comes in last. Emily finishes behind Danny. What was the order of the finish from first to last?

   _____

5. Jean is younger than Dan but older than Rob. Sue is the oldest of the four. Who is the youngest?

   _____

Review and Practice

(Lessons 7 and 9) Write each number in decimal form.

1. 29 hundredths _____

2. 7 hundredths _____

3. 16 thousandths _____

4. 7 tenths _____

5. eight and forty hundredths _____

6. nine and two hundred three thousandths _____

(Lesson 8) In each group circle equivalent decimals.

7. 0.4   0.04   0.40   **8.** 0.02   0.20   0.2

(Lesson 10) Name the number shown by each letter.

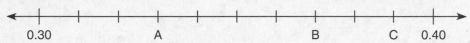

9. A _____   **10.** B _____   **11.** C _____

(Lesson 11) Write >, <, or = to complete.

12. 0.71 ◯ 0.231   **13.** 0.6 ◯ 0.600   **14.** 2.38 ◯ 1.8

15. 6.07 ◯ 6.070   **16.** 0.29 ◯ 0.3   **17.** 5.8 ◯ 6.7

(Lesson 12) Round each number to the place of the underlined digit.

18. 0.6̲51 _____   **19.** 5̲.63 _____

20. Carolyn owes Michael 72¢. She only has dimes.
What is the nearest amount she can give him? _____

(Mixed Review) Write >, <, or =.

21. 6 + 9 + 3 ◯ 9 + 4 + 6   **22.** 18 − 5 ◯ 17 − 4

23. 9 × 3 ◯ 15 + 13   **24.** 5 + 0 ◯ 0 × 8

Estimating Sums and Differences

Estimate each sum or difference.

1. 232 – 75	**2.** $9.67 + 3.44	**3.** 718 +457	**4.** $6.98 – 4.87

5. 728 96 +293	**6.** 382 249 +777	**7.** $11.93 + 2.55	**8.** 599 +607

9. 431 – 65	**10.** $5.68 + 7.55	**11.** 737 +216	**12.** $4.76 – 2.99

13. 525 37 +168	**14.** 345 268 +188	**15.** $9.99 – 4.89	**16.** 699 +103

17. 906 –367	**18.** $6.59 – 3.80	**19.** 608 –398	**20.** $6.78 – 2.80

Estimate. Write >, <, or = to complete.

21. 67 + 49 ◯ 130

22. $16.75 – $7.00 ◯ $23.00

23. 48 + 34 + 95 ◯ 170

24. 444 + 856 ◯ $1,300

25. If you decrease both addends when rounding to add,
what can you say about your estimated sum?

Adding and Subtracting
Whole Numbers

Find each sum or difference. Then estimate to check
your answer.

1. 686
   +208

2. 506
   −331

3. 748
   +992

4.   252
   +3,889

5. 376
   + 49

6. 776
   −634

7. 600
   −277

8. 308
   − 87

9.   47
    599
     23
   + 55

10. 548
    329
    101
   + 88

11. 372 + 65 + 133 + 435 = _____

12. 446 + 9,675 + 11,007 + 329 + 32 = _____

13. Subtract 8,435 from 9,074. _____

14. Find the sum of 4,882, 12,443, 3,229, and 356. _____

15. Find 7,999 + 4,999 mentally. Explain why it is easier
    to do this sum mentally than by writing it out.

    _____

    _____

16. Find 3,000 − 1,002 mentally. Explain your reasoning.

    _____

    _____

17. Find 399 + 598 + 701 mentally. _____

Name _____

Exploring Adding and Subtracting Decimals

Use place-value blocks to add or subtract.

1.   0.3 4
       + 0.5 9

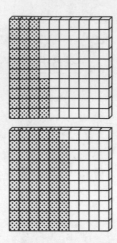

2.   0.6 7
       − 0.5 9

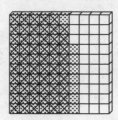

Use place-value blocks or drawings to find each sum
or difference.

3.   4.3 2
       + 5.8 7

4.   5.4 1
       − 1.7 4

5.   5.2 9
       + 8.4 7

6.   4.1
       − 3.7

7.   3.8
       + 5.6

8.   6.8
       + 2.6

9.   9.5 3
       − 4.7 9

10.   1 5.7
        +   0.6

11.   6.2
        + 9.5

12.   8.3 5
        − 0.7 9

13. 4.23 + 5.74 + 6.8 = _____   **14.** 5.9 − 2.8 = _____

Complete. Use place-value blocks or drawings to help you.

15. 4.87 − _____ = 1.23   **16.** 2.35 + _____ = 8.40

17. Explain how you can show 4.37 using dollars, dimes,
and pennies.

_____

_____

Adding Decimals

Find each sum.

1. 6.2 3
+ 8.9 4

2. 4.0 3
+ 5.6 7

3. 4.0 5
+ 0.9 6

4. 5.2 0
+ 0.3 6

5. 6.3 1
+ 7.4 1

6. 4.2 4
0.5 6
+ 3.6 5

7. $3.4 9
0.8 7
+ 2.2 6

8. 0.8 4
2.7 6
+ 0.1 2

9. 4.5 9
2.7 7
+ 6.0

10. 3.9
1.1
+ 8.0

11. $5.2 9
+   0.4 4

12. 6.5
+ 0.4 7

13. 0.6 7
3.2
+ 1.2 5

14. 2.0
3.6 9
+ 2.7 7

15. 4 3.0
+   2.6 0

16. 3.5 + 4.5 + 3 = _____

17. 0.86 + 0.5 = _____

18. 4.6 + 6.7 + 2 = _____

19. 0.73 + 0.48 = _____

20. Find the sum of 4.99 and 3.45. _____

21. Find the sum of 3.9 + 3.09 + 30.9. _____

22. Explain why you cannot write 9.2 as 9.02.

_____

_____

Name _____

Subtracting Decimals

Find each difference.

1. $7.99
  − 4.99

2. 13.0
  − 2.47

3. 35.50
  − 0.87

4. 8.9
  − 0.54

5. 3.33
  − 2.67

6. 14.89
  − 6.55

7. $4.00
  − 3.49

8. 8.9
  − 7.0

9. 5.0
  − 0.6

10. 2.08
  − 0.99

11. $4.44
  − 2.99

12. 4.0
  − 0.67

13. 8.45
  − 4.96

14. 3.98
  − 0.79

15. 14.2
  − 13.27

16. 6.5
  − 0.76

17. 4.7
  − 4.07

18. $9.99
  − 3.68

19. 9.09
  − 5.99

20. $1.00
  − 0.79

21. $8 - 4.65 =$ _____

22. $14.6 - 8.76 =$ _____

23. Find the difference of 7 and 3.64. _____

24. If you have zeros in the tenths and hundredths place in
the first number and fives in the tenths and hundredths
place of the second number, how do you subtract?

_____

_____

Complete.

25. $4.7 -$ _____ $= 0.6$

26. _____ $- 1.75 = 2.68$

Analyze Word Problems:
Choose an Operation

Write the letter of the number sentence you would use.

1. The deluxe soccer gear set costs $55. The regular soccer set costs
$27. What is the difference in costs between the two sets?

   A. $27 + $55 = $82

   B. $55 − $27 = $28

   C. $27 + $82 + $55 = $164

   _____

Write the number sentence or sentences you would use.
Then solve each problem.

2. The special chess set is $14 less than the deluxe chess set,
which costs $68. How much is the special chess set?

   _____

3. Brandon planned on using $80 to buy the deluxe chess set. He
wanted to use his leftover money to buy a book on chess strategy
which costs $10.99. How much money will Brandon have left?

   _____

   _____

4. Brianna had $34 in babysitting money plus $12 allowance. She
would also like to buy the deluxe chess set. How much more money
will she need?

   _____

5. Steven and his sister Jenna want to buy a gift for their parents that
costs $54. Steven has $15 and Jenna has $24. Do they have enough
money to buy the gift? If not, how much more money do they need?

   _____

Name _____

Review and Practice

(Lessons 14 and 15) Find each sum or difference.
Estimate to check.

1.	2.	3.
5 4 4	8 7 8	5 0 2
− 3 9 7	+ 6 6 3	− 4 7

4.	5.	6.
$1 2.1 6	$6 2.9 0	$3 4.0 7
+ 5.0 8	− 2 3.1 7	+ 2 5.2 7

7.	8.	9.
5,0 0 2	1 6,8 9 2	2 4,0 0 0
− 3 5 7	+ 5,3 0 8	− 1 3,5 7 1

(Lessons 16 and 17) Find each sum.

10.	11.	12.	13.
4 2.2 6	$6 2.9 0	9.7	5.2
+ 5.0 8	1 6.8 8	3.7 2	0.3
	+ 3 5.0 2	+ 1.0 8	+ 2 8.1 7

(Lessons 16 and 18) Find each difference.

14.	15.	16.	17.
7.0 3	$1 6.7 5	3.8 1	9
− 3.4 7	− 1 3.5 7	− 0.5	− 1.6 1

(Lesson 19) Choose any strategy to solve the problem.

18. Amy had $15 to buy a CD for $12.95. The tax on the purchase was $0.65. How much money did Amy have left?

_____

(Mixed Review) Multiply.

19. 400 × 2 _____   **20.** 3 × 300 _____

21. 200 × 9 _____   **22.** 4 × 600 _____

Name _____

Cumulative Review

(Chapter 1 Lesson 2) Use the data
from the graph to answer each question.

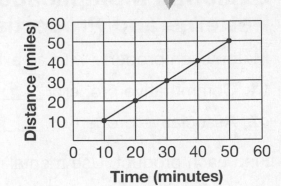

1. How many miles were traveled
in 20 minutes?

_____

2. How many miles would you
expect to travel in 60 minutes? _____

(Chapter 1 Lesson 4) Find the range, median, and mode for
each set of numbers.

3. 10, 12, 12, 9, 3 _____, _____, _____

4. 29, 25, 20, 20, 15, 22 _____, _____, _____

(Chapter 1 Lesson 6) Write a number sentence and use it
to solve the problem.

5. Seth estimates he will need 45 minutes to do his
homework. He needs 15 minutes to do spelling. The rest
of the time he will do his math homework. How many
minutes will Seth spend doing math homework?

_____

(Chapter 2 Lesson 4) Write each number in standard form.

6. three billion, four hundred thirty-six million _____

7. ten billion, five million, six hundred
twenty-one thousand, two hundred thirteen _____

(Chapter 2 Lesson 12) Round each number to the place of
the underlined digit.

8. 45.5̲1 _____   **9.** 0.0̲09 _____   **10.** 3̲.93 _____

(Chapter 2 Lesson 15) Add or subtract.

11.	369	**12.**	371	**13.**	901	**14.**	66,092
	− 197		+ 263		− 38		+ 13,505

Exploring Multiplication Patterns and Properties

Match each property with an example.

1. Commutative property _____   **a.** $6 \times (3 \times 5) = 6 \times (5 \times 3)$

2. Associative property _____   **b.** $4 \times (8 \times 10) = (4 \times 8) \times 10$

Find each product. Use mental math.

3. $20 \times 80 =$ _____   **4.** $6 \times 80 =$ _____

5. $40 \times 40 =$ _____   **6.** $17 \times 20 =$ _____

7. $12 \times (5 \times 10) =$ _____   **8.** $(80 \times 3) \times 20 =$ _____

9. $100 \times (3 \times 90) =$ _____   **10.** $6 \times (60 \times 3) =$ _____

Complete.

11. $40 \times$ _____ $= 1{,}600$ **12.** $30 \times$ _____ $= 900$

13. $50 \times$ _____ $= 30{,}000$ **14.** _____ $\times 80 = 3{,}200$

15. $60 \times$ _____ $= 42{,}000$ **16.** _____ $\times 70 = 700{,}000$

Complete. For each product the factors are the same.

17. _____ $\times$ _____ $= 4{,}900$ **18.** _____ $\times$ _____ $= 250{,}000$

19. _____ $\times$ _____ $= 1{,}600$ **20.** _____ $\times$ _____ $= 90{,}000$

Find each product. Use mental math and multiplication properties.

21. $(22 \times 25) \times 4 =$ _____   **22.** $2 \times (47 \times 5) =$ _____

23. $(2 \times 36) \times 5 =$ _____   **24.** $(60 \times 900) \times 100 =$ _____

25. How many $10 bills are equal to three $20 bills? _____

26. How many zeros are in the product of $4 \times 25 \times 200$? Explain.

_____

27. Which is greater, the product of $50 \times 200 \times 3$ or $5 \times 20 \times 300$? Explain.

_____

_____

Name _____

Practice
3-2

Estimating Products

Estimate each product.

1. 9×34 _____

2. 53×6 _____

3. 8×47 _____

4. 66×4 _____

5. 11×48 _____

6. 37×29 _____

7. 72×31 _____

8. 58×32 _____

9. 19×41 _____

10. 27×433 _____

11. 742×68 _____

12. 77×518 _____

13.
```
   98
 ×21
```

14.
```
   71
 ×63
```

15.
```
  649
 × 42
```

16.
```
  262
 × 68
```

17.
```
  309
 × 47
```

18.
```
  487
 × 31
```

19.
```
   49
 ×49
```

20.
```
  135
 × 77
```

21. Estimate the product of 416 and 72. _____

22. The product of what two numbers is about 400?

_____

23. The product of 42 and what number is about 1,200?

_____

24. The product of what two numbers is about 42,000?

_____

25. The product of 345 and what number is 21,000?

_____

© Scott Foresman Addison Wesley 5

Use with pages 114–115. **39**

Multiplying Whole Numbers

Estimate Find each product. Estimate to check.

1. 66 $\times$ 29	**2.** 95 $\times$ 56	**3.** 73 $\times$ 45	**4.** 83 $\times$ 77	**5.** 115 $\times$ 39

6. $324 \times 8 =$ _____   **7.** $289 \times 5 =$ _____

8. 294 $\times$ 9	**9.** 326 $\times$ 6	**10.** 565 $\times$ 24	**11.** 683 $\times$ 37	**12.** 333 $\times$ 99

13. $24 \times 309 =$ _____   **14.** $41 \times 37 =$ _____

15. 375 $\times$ 9	**16.** 544 $\times$ 6	**17.** 663 $\times$ 24	**18.** 792 $\times$ 36	**19.** 436 $\times$ 87

20. Find the product of 84 and 93. _____

21. Multiply 409 and 37. _____

22. What is the greatest number of times you would regroup when multiplying a 3-digit factor by a 2-digit factor? Give an example.

_____

_____

_____

23. Which is greater, 456×65 or 465×56?

_____

Distributive Property

Find each product.

1. 32 × 9 = _____   **2.** 304 × 8 = _____

3. 5 × 801 = _____   **4.** 698 × 3 = _____

5. 6 × 703 = _____   **6.** 2 × 599 = _____

7. 801 × 9 = _____   **8.** 597 × 7 = _____

9. 29 × 4 = _____   **10.** 42 × 8 = _____

11. 697 × 3 = _____   **12.** 40 × 89 = _____

13. 79 × 12 = _____   **14.** 298 × 11 = _____

15. Multiply 347 and 28. _____

16. Find the product of 80 and 14. _____

17. Would you use the distributive property to find 810 × 9? Explain.

_____

18. Use the distributive property and multiplication patterns
to find 62 × 5 × 10.

_____

_____

Name _____

Choosing a Calculation Method

Choose a method. Find each product.

1. 63
      × 99

2. 800
      × 20

3. 242
      × 87

4. 110
      ×   9

5. 199
      × 33

6. 47
      × 42

7. 490
      × 400

8. 76
      × 67

9. 346 × 56 = _____

10. 290 × 200 = _____

11. 705 × 120 = _____

12. 83 × 15 = _____

13. Find the product of 483 and 264. _____

14. Multiply 204 and 8. _____

15. Jan and her friend each solve 483 multiplied by 276.
Jan's answer is 85,988. Her friend's answer is 133,308.
Which answer is reasonable? Explain.

_____

16. Estimate the product of 52 and 328. Is it closer to
15,000 or 20,000? Explain.

_____

Exploring Patterns with Multiples

This chart shows some multiples of 4 and 5.

| 4 | 4 | 8 | 12 | 20 | 24 | 28 | 32 | 36 | 40 | 44 |
| 5 | 5 | 10 | 15 | 20 | 25 | 30 | 35 | 40 | 45 | 50 |

1. Shade the common multiples of 4 and 5. Which is the least common multiple? _____

Find the LCM for each pair or set of numbers.

2. 3 and 4 _____

3. 5 and 9 _____

4. 2 and 8 _____

5. 6 and 8 _____

6. 2 and 3 _____

7. 7 and 10 _____

8. 10 and 20 _____

9. 3 and 9 _____

10. 9 and 10 _____

11. 5 and 6 _____

12. 4 and 8 _____

13. 2 and 7 _____

14. 2, 4, and 6 _____

15. 3, 5, and 7 _____

16. 2, 4, and 8 _____

17. 2, 5, and 10 _____

18. 3, 6, and 9 _____

19. 2, 3, and 7 _____

20. 3, 4, and 7 _____

21. 2, 3, and 9 _____

22. Use your calculator to find the LCM for 35 and 25. Enter [ON/AC] + 25 [=] [=] and so on. List the multiples. Do the same for 35. What is the first multiple that is a multiple for both 25 and 35?

_____

23. Make a list of the multiples of 30. Do you need to make a list of multiples of 7 to find the LCM of 30 and 7? Explain.

_____

_____

24. What if you want to find the greatest common multiple of 7, 9, and 0? Could you do this? Explain.

_____

_____

Decision Making

A local movie theater sells tickets for $6.00 each and a box of popcorn for $2.00. But if you pay $36.00 for a movie pass, you can see 8 movies in 8 weeks, and get 1 free box of popcorn with each movie. Would you choose to buy the movie pass or not?

What are you asked to do? __Decide whether to get a movie pass or not.__

How much would you have to pay for a ticket and a box of popcorn at the regular price? __$6.00 + $2.00 = $8.00__

How much would each movie and a box of popcorn cost if you got the movie pass? __$36.00 ÷ 8 = $4.50__

About how often would you have to see a movie to go 8 times in 8 weeks? __Once a week__

_____

1. Would it make sense to get the pass if you only go to the movies once or twice in 8 weeks? Explain.

   _____

2. Would it make sense to get the pass if you to go the movies 8 times in 8 weeks? Explain.

   _____

Suppose the same movie theater offered a $12.00 movie pass that allowed you to see 3 movies in the next year.

3. How much would each movie cost? _____

4. How much money would you save if you bought the pass and saw 3 movies that year? _____

5. How much money would you lose if you only saw 1 movie that year? _____

6. Would you buy this movie pass? Explain.

   _____

Name _____

Review and Practice

Vocabulary Fill in each blank with a word from the word bank.

commutative	distributive	least common multiple	multiple

1. $5 \times (3 + 4) = (5 \times 3) + (5 \times 4)$ is an example of

the _____ property.

2. $5 \times 3 = 3 \times 5$ is an example of the _____ property.

3. 16 is a _____ of 2.

4. 48 is the _____ of 16 and 24.

(Lesson 1) Find each product. Use mental math and multiplication properties.

5. $50 \times 3 =$ _____

6. $40 \times 70 =$ _____

7. $60 \times (3 \times 30) =$ _____

8. $80 \times 25 \times 4 =$ _____

(Lesson 2) Estimate each product.

9. 65×27 _____

10. 38×72 _____

11. 81×19 _____

12. 52×94 _____

(Lessons 3–5) Find each product.

13.
$$\begin{array}{r} 584 \\ \times\ \ \ 7 \\ \hline \end{array}$$

14.
$$\begin{array}{r} 98 \\ \times 13 \\ \hline \end{array}$$

15.
$$\begin{array}{r} 92 \\ \times 45 \\ \hline \end{array}$$

16.
$$\begin{array}{r} 705 \\ \times\ \ \ 4 \\ \hline \end{array}$$

17.
$$\begin{array}{r} 600 \\ \times\ 80 \\ \hline \end{array}$$

18.
$$\begin{array}{r} 362 \\ \times\ 42 \\ \hline \end{array}$$

19.
$$\begin{array}{r} 375 \\ \times\ 43 \\ \hline \end{array}$$

20.
$$\begin{array}{r} 481 \\ \times\ 93 \\ \hline \end{array}$$

(Lesson 6) Find the LCM for each set of numbers.

21. 6 and 32 _____

22. 3, 6, and 7 _____

(Mixed Review) Solve.

23. $8 \div 4 \times 6 - 10 =$ _____

24. $4 \times 4 \div 8 + 3 =$ _____

Use with page 132.
45

Name _____

Exploring Decimal Patterns

Draw arrows to show the number of places to move the decimal. Then write the product.

1. 2.38×10 **2.** 2.38×100 **3.** $2.38 \times 1{,}000$

_____   _____   _____

4. 0.356×10 **5.** 0.356×100 **6.** $0.356 \times 1{,}000$

_____   _____   _____

Find each product.

7. $4.7 \times 10 = $ _____   **8.** $0.96 \times 10 = $ _____

     $4.7 \times 100 = $ _____ $0.96 \times 100 = $ _____

     $4.7 \times 1{,}000 = $ _____ $0.96 \times 1{,}000 = $ _____

9. $0.06 \times 10 = $ _____   **10.** $8.437 \times 10 = $ _____

     $0.06 \times 100 = $ _____ $8.437 \times 100 = $ _____

     $0.06 \times 1{,}000 = $ _____ $8.437 \times 1{,}000 = $ _____

Place the decimal point in the product. Write extra zeros if necessary.

11. $1.63 \times 10 = 1\,6\,3$ **12.** $3.72 \times 100 = 3\,7\,2$

13. $0.035 \times 1{,}000 = 3\,5$ **14.** $0.0068 \times 1{,}000 = 6\,8$

15. $1.063 \times 100 = 1\,0\,6\,3$ **16.** $7.04 \times 1{,}000 = 7\,0\,4$

Find each product. Use mental math.

17. $100 \times 2.93 = $ _____   **18.** $1{,}000 \times 3.049 = $ _____

19. $5.47 \times 10 = $ _____   **20.** $8.05 \times 1{,}000 = $ _____

21. $100 \times 0.635 = $ _____   **22.** $10 \times 0.514 = $ _____

23. Money 10 members of the science club each paid $2.50 for a field trip. How much did they pay all together? _____

Estimating Decimal Products

Estimate each product. Explain what you did.

1. 5.2×6 _____

2. 7.8×5 _____

3. 9.1×3 _____

4. 1.7×8 _____

5. 39.7×9 _____

6. 25.1×4 _____

7. 4.19×8 _____

8. 88.9×2 _____

9. 72.3×49 _____

10. 728.1×28 _____

11. 6.6×97 _____

12. 32×511.9 _____

Is each product greater than 250? Write yes or no. Explain.

13. 25.3×8 _____

14. 9×29.97 _____

15. 10×22.19 _____

16. 52.37×5 _____

17. 47.3×6 _____

18. 11×22.3 _____

Is each product greater than 2,500? Write yes or no. Explain.

19. 927.4×2 _____

20. 24.1×99 _____

21. 111×27.43 _____

22. 19.86×198 _____

23. 24.4×100 _____

24. 51.2×51.2 _____

25. Estimate the product of 51.07 and 9.87. _____

26. Estimate the product of 98.57 and 303. _____

27. Estimate the product of 68.9 and 74.2. _____

Name _____

Multiplying Whole Numbers and Decimals

Find each product.

1. $3.14 \times 7 =$ _____

2. $6.05 \times 8 =$ _____

3. $15.45 \times 6 =$ _____

4. $4.51 \times 13 =$ _____

5. $29.4 \times 76 =$ _____

6. $89.03 \times 39 =$ _____

7. $\$15.75 \times 6 =$ _____

8. $\$33.99 \times 4 =$ _____

9. $\$12.45 \times 13 =$ _____

10. $\$21.95 \times 11 =$ _____

11. $\$3.95 \times 24 =$ _____

12. $\$74.63 \times 8 =$ _____

13. $18 \times 347.6 =$ _____

14. $93 \times 72.6 =$ _____

15. $9 \times \$26.37 =$ _____

16. $6 \times \$147.50 =$ _____

Choose the number that is closest to the actual product.

17. $\$3.25 \times 11$ _____ **A.** $300 **B.** $50 **C.** $30

18. $\$6.80 \times 39$ _____ **A.** $28 **B.** $280 **C.** $180

19. $\$4.75 \times 22$ _____ **A.** $1,000 **B.** $100 **C.** $80

20. 2.008×100 _____ **A.** 20 **B.** 2,000 **C.** 200

21. What is the product of 7.09 and 16? _____

22. What is the product of $1.85 and 34? _____

23. Bill says the product of 6 and 3.79 is 227.4. Is he correct? Explain.

_____

_____

24. Circle each multiplication sentence whose product is a whole number.

3×45.7 12.2×5 6×8.5 7.6×4

23.5×45 6.15×4 5×32.8 4×7.25

Analyzing Word Problems:
Multiple-Step Problems

Solve each problem.

1. Sandwiches at the diner are $3.75, a salad costs $1.19, and a glass of juice costs $0.99. A family went to the diner and ordered 3 sandwiches, 2 salads, and 3 glasses of juice.

   a. How much will the family pay for the 3 sandwiches? _____

   b. How much will the family pay for the 2 salads? _____

   c. How much will the family pay for the 3 glasses of juice? _____

   d. How much is the total bill? _____

Solve each problem. Chose any strategy.

2. The hobby shop sells many different varieties of kites. Box kites are $6.69, diamonds are $5.95, and dragon kites are $11.98.

   a. Mr. Sanders bought 2 box kites and 2 diamond kites for his 4 children. How much did he spend? _____

   b. Ms. Byars bought 3 box kites and 2 dragon kites for her 5 children. How much did she spend? _____

3. A video store charges $2.50 for new movies and $1.50 for children's movies. If a family rents 2 new movies and 3 children's movies, how much will they pay? _____

4. At a state fair, the Lanier family had 120 jars of their homemade jelly to sell. Large jars were $4.50 each and small jars were $2.50 each.

   a. How much would you pay if you bought 3 large jars and 4 small ones? _____

   b. By the end of the day, the Laniers sold 40 large jars of jelly. They made $330 in all. How much did they make selling small jars of jelly? _____

   c. How many small jars of jelly did they sell? _____

   d. How many jars did the Laniers have leftover? _____

Name _____

Review and Practice

Vocabulary Underline the word that correctly to completes the sentence.

1. 4 and 25 are (compatible, decimal) numbers for multiplication.

2. The product of 0.23 and 10 is a (compatible, decimal) number.

(Lesson 8) Find each product.

3. $6.04 \times 10 =$ _____

4. $1.85 \times 100 =$ _____

5. $0.92 \times 100 =$ _____

6. $0.0065 \times 1,000 =$ _____

7. $1.98 \times 10 =$ _____

8. $0.0236 \times 1,000 =$ _____

(Lesson 9) Estimate each product.

9. 16×8.46 _____

10. 6.12×82 _____

11. 307×9.5 _____

12. 4.78×30 _____

13. 25×0.12 _____

14. 1.11×73 _____

(Lesson 10) Use estimation to place the decimal point in each product.

15. $6.15 \times 98 = 6\ 0\ 2\ 7$

16. $9.82 \times 35 = 3\ 4\ 3\ 7$

17. $52.7 \times 23 = 1\ 2\ 1\ 2\ 1$

18. $11.1 \times 49 = 5\ 4\ 3\ 9$

19. $\$1.23 \times 9 = \$1\ 1\ 0\ 7$

20. $\$6.88 \times 707 = \$4\ 8\ 6\ 4\ 1\ 6$

(Lesson 11) Solve each problem.

21. A granola bar sells for $0.55. An eight-pack of the same bars costs $4.00. How much could you save on a purchase of an eight-pack? _____

22. A candle maker can make 3 candles from 6 pounds of wax. How many pounds of wax would be needed to make 15 of the same candles? _____

(Mixed Review) Multiply or divide.

23. $3 \times 8 =$ _____

24. $45 \div 9 =$ _____

25. $42 \div 7 =$ _____

26. $5 \times 7 =$ _____

27. $8 \times 9 =$ _____

28. $36 \div 6 =$ _____

Exploring Decimal Multiplication

1. Use the 10 × 10 grid to show 0.7 of 0.9.

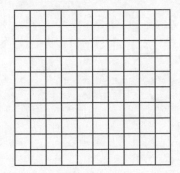

   a. Use yellow to shade 0.7 on the grid as 7 rows.

   b. Use blue to shade 0.9 on the grid as 9 columns.

   c. Count the green squares. 0.7 of 0.9 is _____.

Find each product. You can use 10 × 10 grids to help.

2. 0.4 of 0.5   **3.** 0.3 of 0.7   **4.** 0.4 of 0.7   **5.** 0.9 of 0.2

_____   _____   _____   _____

6. 0.8 of 0.5   **7.** 0.8 of 0.9   **8.** 0.8 of 0.6   **9.** 0.3 of 0.6

_____   _____   _____   _____

10. 0.6 of 0.6   **11.** 0.4 of 0.6   **12.** 0.6 of 0.3   **13.** 0.8 of 0.7

_____   _____   _____   _____

14. 0.5 of 0.6   **15.** 0.3 of 0.9   **16.** 0.4 of 0.1   **17.** 0.9 of 0.9

_____   _____   _____   _____

18. Find the product of 0.7 and 0.7. _____

19. The product is 0.64. One of the
factors is 0.8. What is the other factor? _____

20. Write two numbers whose product is 0.35. _____

21. Write two numbers whose product is 0.49. _____

22. A can of dog food weighs 0.6 lb. Arthur's dog gets 0.5 can
of food for dinner. How much does the dog's dinner weigh?

_____

Name _____

Multiplying Decimals by Decimals

Find each product. Round to the nearest cent when necessary.

1.   3.4 5
    ×   0.4

2. $7.1 0
    ×   4 2

3.   1.4 5
    ×   4.5

4. $4 3.3 8
    ×   1.6 5

5.   3.8 1
    × 4.1 2 1

6.   6.0 9
    ×   5.4

7.   0.0 9 1
    ×   7 4.4

8.   4.7 9 9
    ×   5

9.   2 3 1
    × 0.3 0 1

10. $1 7.3 2
    ×   0.0 4

11.   3.5
    × 3.5

12. $1 2.3 0
    ×   4

13. Find the product of 49.3 and 0.22. _____

14. Find the product of $8.43 and 24.5. Round to the nearest cent.

_____

15. The product of 4,005 × 6,004 is 24,046,020. What is the product of 4.005 and 6.004?

_____

16. Without doing the multiplication, tell how many decimal places are in the product of 4.97 and 3.456.

_____

17. Without doing the multiplication, tell how many decimal places are in the product of 72.35 and 14.12.

_____

Finding High and Low Estimates

Between which two numbers will each product be found?

1. 8.6×8.762 _____

    A. 8 and 9   **B.** 16 and 48   **C.** 64 and 81

2. 7.9×5.23 _____

    A. 7 and 5   **B.** 57 and 75   **C.** 35 and 48

3. 9.6×0.74 _____

    A. 9 and 16   **B.** 0 and 10   **C.** 9 and 63

Estimate low and high. Then find each product.

4. $5.4 \times 6 =$ _____   **5.** $41.3 \times 7 =$ _____

    Estimate: Estimate:

    _____   _____

6. $9.3 \times 4 =$ _____   **7.** $7.8 \times 3 =$ _____

    Estimate: Estimate

    _____   _____

8.   1 4.4   **9.**   4.9   **10.**   6.9   **11.**   7.9
    $\times$ 6.2 $\times$ 8.1 $\times$ 3.2 $\times$ 8.3

    Estimate: Estimate: Estimate: Estimate

    _____   _____   _____   _____

12. Estimate low and high. Then find the product of 89.4 and 4.8.

_____

13. What 2 decimal factors when multiplied
result in a product between 15 and 24? _____

14. How can you use estimation to know that the product of
4.5 and 6.89 is more than 24?

_____

Decimals and Zeros

Find each product. Write zeros where needed.

1. $0.2 \times 0.3 =$ _____

2. $7.2 \times 0.0007 =$ _____

3. $1.25 \times 0.05 =$ _____

4. $0.004 \times 0.08 =$ _____

5. $3.4 \times 0.0006 =$ _____

6. $0.04 \times 0.04 =$ _____

7. $5.05 \times 4.02 =$ _____

8. $0.08 \times 10.05 =$ _____

9. 0.008
$\times 0.004$

10. 0.07
$\times 0.006$

11. 8.9
$\times 0.003$

12. 2.1
$\times 0.08$

13. 12
$\times 0.005$

14. 0.045
$\times 0.004$

15. 7.005
$\times \quad 0.06$

16. 5.05
$\times 5.04$

17. 12.4
$\times 0.004$

18. 18.4
$\times 0.0002$

19. 9.3
$\times 0.0044$

20. 76
$\times 0.0003$

21. Find the product of 0.25 and 3.9. _____

22. Find the product of 6.2 and 0.4. _____

23. Is the product of 0.006 and 1.5 greater or less than 1.5?
Explain.

_____

_____

Analyzing Strategies: Guess and Check

Use the Guess and Check strategy to solve each problem.

Two owners compared the weights of their dogs. Together, the two dogs weigh 36 lb. The spaniel weighs 6 lb more than the poodle.

1. What is a reasonable first guess for the weight of the poodle?

_____

2. The two dogs together weigh 36 lb. Is it possible for the spaniel to weigh 24 lb? Explain.

_____

3. How much did each dog weigh?

_____

Use Guess and Check or any strategy to help solve each problem.

4. Together, Fred and Frank have been working 25 years. Frank has worked 7 years longer than Fred. How many years has each been working?

_____

5. The cross country team is planning a 30 km relay. Each team member will run either 4 or 6 km. The same number of team members will run each distance. How many team members will run each distance?

_____

6. At the hardware store, doorbells cost $12, while doorknobs cost $8. Greg's Refinishing Company spent $120 on 12 items. How many of each item did they buy?

_____

7. Lawrence has $10. He gets a $6 a week allowance for doing household chores. How many weeks will it take him to save for a video game that costs $52?

_____

Review and Practice

(Lesson 12) Place a decimal in each product.

1. $0.4 \times 0.7 = 0\ 2\ 8$

2. $0.08 \times 5 = 0\ 4\ 0$

3. $0.2 \times 0.9 = 0\ 1\ 8$

3. $0.15 \times 9 = 0\ 1\ 3\ 5$

(Lesson 13) Find each product. Round to the nearest cent when necessary.

5.
```
  14.4
×  6.2
```

6.
```
  4.9
× 8.1
```

7.
```
$ 6.9 0
×    3.2
```

8.
```
  7.9
× 8.3
```

(Lesson 14) Between which two numbers will each product be found?

9. 3.91×0.95 _____ **A.** 1 and 3 **B.** 3 and 4 **C.** 4 and 5

10. 6.6×9.2 _____ **A.** 54 and 70 **B.** 40 and 54 **C.** 6 and 9

11. 9.43×7.99 _____ **A.** 7 and 9 **B.** 56 and 63 **C.** 63 and 80

(Lesson 15) Find each product. Insert zeros where necessary.

12.
```
   3.0 0 9
× 0.0 0 2 8
```

13.
```
  8.5 9
× 1.0 1
```

14.
```
0.0 0 0 3 8
×      0.0 5
```

(Lesson 16) Solve.

15. Sandro's skateboard cost $8 more than Kim's. Together their skateboards cost $80. How much did each pay for their skateboards?

_____

(Mixed Review) Add or subtract.

16.
```
  7 3.5
+   3.5
```

17.
```
  3 6.8 1
+    3.5
```

18.
```
  1 2 2.8 9
−    3 2.9 8
```

19.
```
  $2 3.0 0
−     5.9 9
```

Cumulative Review

(Chapter 1 Lesson 10) Use the data to answer 1 and 2.

Number of Sit-ups in Gym Class									
23	24	15	16	23	30	30	14	22	33
13	19	20	30	32	30	20	10	22	23

1. Make a stem-and-leaf plot for the number of sit-ups in gym class.

2. What is the median, range, and mode of the number of sit-ups?

_____

(Chapter 2 Lesson 9) Write each number in decimal form.

3. 8 thousandths _____   4. 40 hundredths _____

5. three hundred one thousandths _____

(Chapter 2 Lesson 18) Subtract.

6. $3.6 9
   − 1.9 7

7. 9.7 1
   − 2.0 3

8. 6.0 1
   − 3

9. 8
   − 1.3 5

(Chapter 3 Lesson 3) Find each product.

10. 2 6 7
    ×   5

11. 6 1 2
    ×   6

12. 5 0 1
    ×   3

13. 7 3 6
    ×   8

(Chapter 3 Lesson 6) Find the LCM for each set of numbers.

14. 3 and 7 _____   15. 5, 6, and 10 _____

(Chapter 3 Lesson 15) Find each product. Insert zeros where necessary.

16. 2.0 1 9
    × 0.0 0 5

17. 1.5 6 7
    × 0.0 1 6

18. 0.0 0 0 0 4 3
    ×   0.0 3

Reviewing the Meaning of Division

Find each quotient.

1. 56 ÷ 7 = _____   **2.** 42 ÷ 6 = _____   **3.** 24 ÷ 4 = _____

4. 32 ÷ 8 = _____   **5.** 30 ÷ 5 = _____   **6.** 54 ÷ 6 = _____

7. 36 ÷ 6 = _____   **8.** 21 ÷ 3 = _____   **9.** 35 ÷ 7 = _____

10. 72 ÷ 9 = _____   **11.** 36 ÷ 4 = _____   **12.** 15 ÷ 5 = _____

13. 12 ÷ 3 = _____   **14.** 64 ÷ 8 = _____   **15.** 49 ÷ 7 = _____

16. Identify each number in the equations 7 × 4 = 28 and
28 ÷ 7 = 4 as a factor, a product, a divisor, a dividend,
or a quotient.

7	×	4	=	28
↓		↓		↓
_____		_____		_____

28	÷	7	=	4
↓		↓		↓
_____		_____		_____

17. If you know that 6 × 3 = 18, you also know that
3 × 6 = 18. Solve for n

a. 18 ÷ 6 = n _____

b. 18 ÷ 3 = n _____

18. Laura's uncle would not tell his age. Instead he gave
some clues: "When you divide my age by 5, the quotient
is less than 9. I am younger than 55 but older than 35."
What is his age?

_____

Exploring Patterns to Divide

Complete the patterns.

1. 36 ÷ 4 = _____

360 ÷ 4 = _____

3,600 ÷ 4 = _____

36,000 ÷ 4 = _____

2. 42 ÷ 7 = _____

420 ÷ 7 = _____

4,200 ÷ 7 = _____

42,000 ÷ 7 = _____

3. 64 ÷ 8 = _____

640 ÷ 8 = _____

6,400 ÷ 8 = _____

64,000 ÷ 8 = _____

4. 20 ÷ 5 = _____

200 ÷ 5 = _____

2,000 ÷ 5 = _____

20,000 ÷ 5 = _____

Use patterns and basic facts to divide mentally.

5. 27 ÷ 9 = _____

6. 270 ÷ 9 = _____

7. 3,600 ÷ 6 = _____

8. 12,000 ÷ 2 = _____

9. 350 ÷ 5 = _____

10. 1,500 ÷ 3 = _____

11. 49,000 ÷ 7 = _____

12. 7,200 ÷ 8 = _____

Complete.

13. 1,800 ÷ ☐ = 600

14. ☐ ÷ 6 = 80

15. 21,000 ÷ ☐ = 3,000

16. 400 ÷ ☐ = 80

17. ☐ ÷ 4 = 400

18. 24,000 ÷ ☐ = 8,000

Estimating Quotients

Estimate each quotient.

1. 635 ÷ 9 _____   **2.** 233 ÷ 6 _____

3. 371 ÷ 6 _____   **4.** 517 ÷ 7 _____

5. 386 ÷ 5 _____   **6.** 145 ÷ 8 _____

7. 163 ÷ 3 _____   **8.** 801 ÷ 9 _____

9. 117 ÷ 2 _____   **10.** 468 ÷ 9 _____

11. 554 ÷ 7 _____   **12.** 354 ÷ 4 _____

13. Estimate the quotient of 203 ÷ 6. _____

14. Estimate the quotient of 391 ÷ 8. _____

15. Estimate the quotient of 264 ÷ 3. _____

16. You know that 481 ÷ 7 is about 70. Is the exact quotient
greater than or less than the estimate? Find estimates
for 4,810 ÷ 7, 48,100 ÷ 7, and 48 ÷ 7.

_____

17. You know that 332 ÷ 4 is about 80. Find estimates for
33 ÷ 4 and 33,200 ÷ 4.

_____

18. You know that 351 ÷ 6 is about 60. Find estimates for
3,510 ÷ 6 and 35,100 ÷ 6.

_____

Name _____

Review and Practice

Vocabulary Use the example to answer each question.

1. Which number is the quotient? _____
2. Which number is the dividend? _____
3. Which number is the divisor? _____
4. Which number is the remainder? _____

$$3\overline{)28} \quad \begin{array}{r} 9\ R1 \end{array}$$

(Lesson 1) Find each quotient. Use mental math.

5. $24 \div 3 =$ _____
6. $25 \div 5 =$ _____
7. $36 \div 9 =$ _____
8. $56 \div 8 =$ _____

9. Whitney poured 36 ounces of juice in 6 glasses. How many ounces of juice are in each glass? _____

(Lesson 2) Find each quotient. Use mental math.

10. $4,500 \div 9 =$ _____
11. $40,000 \div 5 =$ _____
12. $1,200 \div 2 =$ _____
13. $540 \div 6 =$ _____

Complete.

14. $14,000 \div$ _____ $= 7,000$
15. _____ $\div 8 = 30$

(Lesson 3) Estimate each quotient by substituting compatible numbers.

16. $163 \div 2$ _____
17. $459 \div 9$ _____
18. $761 \div 8$ _____
19. $358 \div 4$ _____

(Mixed Review) Add or subtract.

20.
$$\begin{array}{r} 6,512 \\ +\ \ 739 \\ \hline \end{array}$$

21.
$$\begin{array}{r} 3,003 \\ -1,439 \\ \hline \end{array}$$

22.
$$\begin{array}{r} 117 \\ -\ 99 \\ \hline \end{array}$$

23.
$$\begin{array}{r} 997 \\ +\ 53 \\ \hline \end{array}$$

Exploring Dividing

Complete. You may use play money to help.

```
      $□.3□ R□
1. 7)$9.28
     -7
      □2
     -□□
       1□
      -14
        □
```

```
      $□.9□ R□
2. 3)$8.93
     -□
      29
     -□□
       □3
      -21
        □
```

3. 4)$9.53　　**4.** 6)$8.75　　**5.** 2)$3.72　　**6.** 7)$7.94

7. 3)$4.36　　**8.** 3)$9.34　　**9.** 5)$8.97　　**10.** 4)$6.41

Dividing by 1-Digit Divisors

Divide.

1. 96 ÷ 4 _____   **2.** 622 ÷ 5 _____

3. 473 ÷ 2 _____   **4.** 547 ÷ 3 _____

5. 2)483   **6.** 7)247   **7.** 3)881   **8.** 8)964

9. 2)726   **10.** 4)973   **11.** 5)362   **12.** 4)739

13. Estimate the quotient for 735 ÷ 3. What number
is in the hundreds place in the quotient?

_____

14. When dividing a 3-digit number by a 1-digit number, for
what divisors can you get a remainder of 8? Explain.

_____

Analyze Word Problems:
Interpret Remainders

Solve. Use the picture to answer **1–3**.

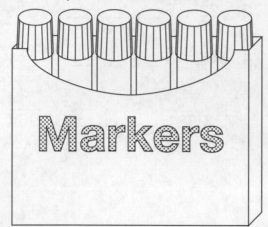

1. If you need markers for a class of 28 students, how many full boxes will you use? _____

2. How many more markers will you need after using the full boxes? _____

3. If you opened enough boxes to supply the entire class with markers, how many boxes would you open? _____

4. In the store room, folders are stored in packages of 8. What is the least number of packages needed for a class of 35 students? _____

5. The cafeteria workers keep small milk cartons in the refrigerator in stacks of 6. If each worker carries no more than one stack, what is the least number of cafeteria workers needed to carry small milk cartons for a class of 32?

_____

6. In the cafeteria's refrigerator, cups of yogurt are kept in stacks of 9. If each worker carries no more than one stack, what is the least number of workers needed to carry cups of yogurt for a class of 42?

_____

7. In the teachers' lunchroom, teachers sit at tables for 6. There are 22 teachers eating lunch. How many tables must be set up?

_____

Deciding Where to Place the First Digit

Divide. Check your answer.

1. 7)381

2. 5)208

3. 6)682

4. 8)329

5. 4)173

6. 8)484

7. 5)571

8. 4)925

9. 6)674

10. 317 ÷ 4 = _____

11. 815 ÷ 7 = _____

12. 997 ÷ 3 = _____

13. 411 ÷ 9 = _____

14. 859 ÷ 4 = _____

15. 371 ÷ 7 = _____

16. Divide 723 by 5. _____

17. Find 673 divided by 4. _____

18. The divisor is 6 and the dividend is 752. Divide. _____

19. The divisor is 9 and the dividend is 255. Divide. _____

Zeros in the Quotient

Divide. Multiply to check.

1. 6)242 **2.** 3)90 **3.** 7)213

4. 9)918 **5.** 5)2,004 **6.** 3)627

7. 4)8,012 **8.** 6)2,460 **9.** 5)3,015

10. 7)709 **11.** 8)2,408 **12.** 6)1,892

13. 5)2,205 **14.** 3)1,229 **15.** 9)6,311

Use mental math to find each quotient.

16. $360 \div 6 =$ _____ **17.** $5,600 \div 8 =$ _____

18. $42,000 \div 7 =$ _____ **19.** $180 \div 3 =$ _____

20. $48,000 \div 8 =$ _____ **21.** $15,000 \div 5 =$ _____

22. Divide 965 by 9. _____

23. Are there any zeros in the quotient of $495 \div 4$? How can
you tell without finding the quotient?

_____

Name _____

Exploring Mean

Complete each sentence using a word from the word bank.

56   64   72   72   81   83   97

1. The _____ is 72 because it is the number that appears most.

2. To find the _____, add all the numbers and divide by 7.

3. The _____ is 72 because it is the middle number.

| mean |
| median |
| mode |

Find the mean, median, and mode for each set of data.

4. 115, 124, 130, 122, 124

   _____, _____, _____

5. $5.26, $5.50, $4.87, $4.04, $6.21, $5.26,

   _____, _____, _____

6. $7.08, $7.78, $8.07, $8.70, $8.87

   _____, _____, _____

7. Find the mean, median, and mode for the set of data in the bar graph.

   _____

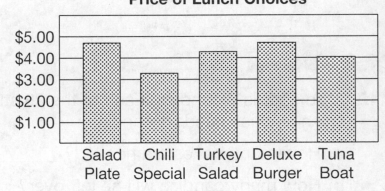

Price of Lunch Choices

8. Can the median of a set of numbers ever be the greatest number in the set of data? Explain.

_____

_____

9. Suppose you wanted to find the mean, median, and mode of 55, 56, 57, 58, 59. How could you find them mentally?

_____

_____

Name _____

Review and Practice

Vocabulary Fill in each blank with a word from the word bank.

| mean   median   mode |

1. The _____ is the middle number of an ordered set of numbers.

2. The _____ is the average of a set of numbers.

3. The _____ is the most common value in a set of data.

(Lessons 4, 5, 7, and 8) Divide. Multiply to check your answer.

4. $15.50 ÷ 5 = _____   **5.** $9.68 ÷ 8 = _____

6. 6)2,406   **7.** 7)287   **8.** 3)762

9. 4)4,191   **10.** 8)417   **11.** 9)3,687

12. A box holds 7 candles. Each of the 29 students in
science class needs 1 candle.

    a. How many boxes are needed? _____

    b. How many candles will be left over? _____

(Lesson 9) Find the mean, median, and mode for each set of data.

13. 15, 17, 15, 11, 12   _____, _____, _____

14. 5, 8, 8, 10, 11, 6   _____, _____, _____

15. $27, $36, $51, $42, $36, $48   _____, _____, _____

(Mixed Review) Add.

16. 7 + 5 + 2 + 8 = _____   **17.** 1 + 8 + 2 + 9 = _____

Exploring Products and Quotients

Match each number sentence with the property it shows.

_____ **1.** $6 \times 9 = 9 \times 6$ **a.** Zero property

_____ **2.** $729 \times 1 = 729$ **b.** One property

_____ **3.** $(8 \times 3) \times 4 = 8 \times (3 \times 4)$ **c.** Commutative property

_____ **4.** $0 \times 1,267 = 0$ **d.** Associative property

Complete. Write >, <, or =.

5. $23 \times 6 = n$ **a.** $n \bigcirc 23$ **b.** $n \bigcirc 6$

6. $36 \div 3 = n$ **a.** $n \bigcirc 36$ **b.** $n \bigcirc 3$

7. $17,549 \times 1 = n$ **a.** $n \bigcirc 17,549$ **b.** $n \bigcirc 1$

8. $n \div 8 = 0$ **a.** $n \bigcirc 8$ **b.** $n \bigcirc 0$

9. $4,195 \div 1 = n$ **a.** $n \bigcirc 4,195$ **b.** $n \bigcirc 1$

10. $157 \div 5 = 31 \text{ R } n$ **a.** $n \bigcirc 157$ **b.** $n \bigcirc 5$

Write whether each equation is true or false. Explain how you know.

11. $45 \div 9 = 9 \div 45$ _____

12. $0 \times 14,275 = 0$ _____

13. $587 \div 587 = 1$ _____

14. $0 \div 4,113 = 4,113$ _____

15. $81 \div 9 = 9 \div 81$ _____

16. $24 \times 3 = 3 \times 24$ _____

17. Peter said he divided 7 into a number and got zero.
What is the number? Explain how you know.

_____

Dividing Money

Find each quotient. Multiply to check.

1. 7)$42.00

2. 4)$4.04

3. 3)$13.32

4. 5)$25.15

5. 6)$34.32

6. 7)$71.89

7. 3)$182.10

8. 5)$325.35

9. 8)$469.44

Use a calculator to divide. Write each answer to the nearest cent.

10. $5.11 ÷ 4 = _____

11. $12.77 ÷ 5 = _____

12. 7)$898.13

13. 8)$73.45

14. 6)$2,014.10

15. 3)$745.31

16. For $42.01 ÷ 2, $297.66 ÷ 6, and $8.43 ÷ 8, are any of the quotients less than a dollar? How can you tell?

_____

_____

Dividing Decimals

Find each quotient.

1. 4)$\overline{25.424}$ **2.** 6)$\overline{16.032}$ **3.** 5)$\overline{33.195}$

4. 9)$\overline{59.283}$ **5.** 8)$\overline{18.512}$ **6.** 3)$\overline{31.701}$

7. 7)$\overline{8.169}$ **8.** 2)$\overline{14.948}$ **9.** 5)$\overline{22.325}$

Find the length of the side of each square.

10.

```
Perimeter =
12.744 cm
```

11.

```
Perimeter =
26.108 m
```

_____   _____

12. Is 66.781 ÷ 7 = 22.903 a reasonable answer? Explain
why or why not.

_____

_____

Factors and Divisibility

Find the factors for each number.

1. 25 _____

2. 12 _____

3. 21 _____

4. 40 _____

5. 36 _____

6. 45 _____

7. 49 _____

8. 33 _____

9. 30 _____

10. 56 _____

11. What are the factors of 65? _____

12. What are the factors of 28? _____

13. What are the factors of 32? _____

14. What are the factors of 27? _____

15. Is 3 a factor of 261? Explain how you know.

_____

16. Is 10 a factor of 325? Explain how you know.

_____

17. Is 6 a factor of 492? Explain how you know.

_____

_____

_____

Exploring Prime and Composite Numbers

Complete each sentence using a word from the word bank.

composite number
factors
factor tree
prime number
products

1. A _____ has exactly two different factors.

2. 21 is an example of a

_____.

3. You can use a _____ to show the factors of a composite number.

4. A composite number has more than two _____.

Write whether each number is prime or composite.

5. 38 _____   **6.** 19 _____   **7.** 83 _____

Use factor trees to find the prime factors of each number.

8. 12   **9.** 32   **10.** 30

Write the missing factors.

11. 1, ⬚, ⬚, 4, ⬚ 12   **12.** 1, ⬚, 49

13. Can a whole number ending in 8 be prime? Explain. _____

_____

Analyze Strategies: Work Backward

Work backward to solve each problem.

1. On Sundays, Bernie's Bagel shop gets very busy. Two hours
after they opened, Bernie's sold one third of their bagels. During the
next hour, they sold another 50 bagels. During the rest of the day,
half of the remaining bagels were bought. At closing, there were only
25 bagels left.

   a. How many bagels were left at closing? _____

   b. What operation undoes dividing the number of bagels in half?

     _____

   c. What operation undoes subtracting 50? _____

   d. How many bagels were in the store when it opened on Sunday?

     _____

Use any strategy to solve each problem.

2. Arlene keeps track of her weekly expenses. At the end of a week,
she had $2.35 left. She had bought 2 bottles of juice for $0.80
each and one package of markers for $4.55. How much did Arlene
have at the beginning of the week?

   _____

3. The tag on the shirt shows that the
price has been lowered twice. What
was the original price of the shirt?

   _____

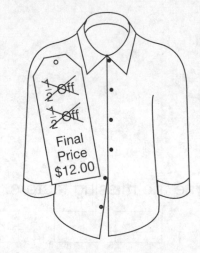

4. Louis had homework in 2 subjects. He finished his homework at
6:00 P.M. He spent 30 minutes doing his science homework. He spent
twice that amount of time doing his reading homework. At what time
did Louis start his homework?

   _____

Review and Practice

Vocabulary Write true or false for each statement.

1. A whole number greater than 1 that has more
than two different factors is a composite number. _____

2. Any number that divides another number
with a remainder of 2 is called a factor. _____

(Lesson 10) Complete.

3. _____ ÷ 678 = 0   **4.** 389 × _____ = 389

(Lesson 11) Find each quotient. Round to the nearest cent.

5. $3\overline{)\$16.00}$ **6.** $7\overline{)\$125.10}$ **7.** $4\overline{)\$8.31}$

(Lesson 12) Find each quotient.

8. $2\overline{)13.162}$ **9.** $6\overline{)37.662}$ **10.** $7\overline{)8.491}$

(Lesson 13) Find all the factors for each number.

11. 8 _____   **12.** 18 _____

13. 36 _____

(Lesson 14) Use factor trees to find the prime factors of each number.

14. 20   **15.** 31   **16.** 50

(Mixed Review) Find each sum or difference.

17. 426 + 238 = _____   **18.** 204 − 97 = _____

Cumulative Review

(Chapter 2 Lesson 18) Subtract.

1. $23.12
     −   8.97

2. 0.71
     − 0.46

3. $5.00
     − 3.99

4. 3
     − 1.35

(Chapter 3 Lesson 13) Find each product.

5. 2.67
     × 0.5

6. $6.12
     ×   26

7. 4.81
     × 7.3

8. 8.36
     × 0.58

(Chapter 3 Lesson 15) Find each product. Insert zeros where necessary.

9. 1.075
     × 0.003

10. 1.092
      × 0.006

11.   2.3
      × 0.00008

(Chapter 4 Lessons 7, 8, and 12) Find each quotient.

12. 5)69

13. 9)369

14. 7)1,456

15. 4)820

16. 8)4,809

17. 3)9,245

18. 6)19.404

19. 2)6.238

20. 9)37.926

Name _____

Exploring Division Patterns

You can use number sense and basic facts to divide with multiples of 10.

1. a. What basic fact would you use to find 810 ÷ 90? _____

   b. 810 ÷ 90 = _____

2. a. What basic fact would you use to find 42,000 ÷ 70? _____

   b. 42,000 ÷ 70 = _____

Find each quotient. Use mental math.

3. 2,400 ÷ 60 = _____   **4.** 2,700 ÷ 90 = _____

5. 350 ÷ 50 = _____   **6.** 1,800 ÷ 300 = _____

7. 32,000 ÷ 80 = _____   **8.** 60,000 ÷ 200 = _____

9. 4,000 ÷ 500 = _____   **10.** 63,000 ÷ 70 = _____

11. 1,600 ÷ 40 = _____   **12.** 720 ÷ 90 = _____

Complete.

13. 1,200 ÷ _____ = 40   **14.** 24,000 ÷ _____ = 80

15. _____ ÷ 500 = 50   **16.** _____ ÷ 80 = 800

For each pair, write whether the quotient is the same or different. Explain.

17. 500 ÷ 50 and 5,000 ÷ 500

_____

18. 240 ÷ 3 and 24,000 ÷ 30

_____

19. How would you find 49,000 ÷ 7?

_____

_____

Estimating Quotients: High and Low

Estimate each quotient. Give a high and low estimate.

1. 16,786 ÷ 50

_____

2. $26,521 ÷ 30

_____

3. 4,033 ÷ 60

_____

4. 6,945 ÷ 80

_____

5. 22,487 ÷ 40

_____

6. $33,132 ÷ 70

_____

7. 5,399 ÷ 80

_____

8. 13,452 ÷ 30

_____

9. 3,000 ÷ 90

_____

10. 4,465 ÷ 60

_____

11. 57,029 ÷ 70

_____

12. 1,553 ÷ 20

_____

13. $3,909 ÷ 50

_____

14. 2,517 ÷ 40

_____

15. 14,129 ÷ 30

_____

16. 57,221 ÷ 60

_____

17. 4,417 ÷ 50

_____

18. 26,951 ÷ 80

_____

19. How is estimating the quotient of 4,740 and 60 similar to estimating the quotient of 474,000 and 600?

_____

_____

20. How is estimating the quotient of 6,840 and 90 similar to estimating the quotient of 684,000 and 9,000?

_____

_____

Estimating with 2-Digit Divisors

Estimate each quotient using compatible numbers.

1. 821 ÷ 18

_____

2. 592 ÷ 33

_____

3. 3,465 ÷ 49

_____

4. 809 ÷ 92

_____

5. 7,468 ÷ 82

_____

6. $24,424 ÷ 59

_____

7. 585 ÷ 58

_____

8. 21,000 ÷ 74

_____

9. $557 ÷ 83

_____

10. 362 ÷ 51

_____

11. 4,106 ÷ 55

_____

12. $8,123 ÷ 20

_____

13. 32,128 ÷ 36

_____

14. $1,107 ÷ 21

_____

15. 3,727 ÷ 45

_____

16. Estimate the quotient of 989 ÷ 48. Is the exact quotient greater than or less than your estimate?

_____

17. Estimate the quotient of 607 ÷ 22. Is the exact quotient greater than or less than your estimate?

_____

18. Which quotient is greater: 4,322 ÷ 18 or 4,322 ÷ 19? _____

19. Which quotient is greater: 1,868 ÷ 32 or 1,868 ÷ 27? _____

Review and Practice

Vocabulary Write true or false for each statement.

1. Six is the quotient. _____

2. 17 is the dividend. _____

$$\begin{array}{r} 2\ R5 \\ 6\overline{)17} \end{array}$$

(Lesson 1) Find each quotient. Use mental math.

3. 1,800 ÷ 30 = _____   4. 24,000 ÷ 80 = _____

5. 450 ÷ 90 = _____   6. 5,600 ÷ 700 = _____

7. Are the quotients for 560 ÷ 8 and
56,000 ÷ 80 the same or different? _____

(Lesson 2) Estimate each quotient. Give a high and low estimate.

8. 16,993 ÷ 20   9. 49,695 ÷ 90

_____   _____

10. 7,613 ÷ 80   11. 35,800 ÷ 60

_____   _____

(Lesson 3) Estimate each quotient by using compatible numbers.

12. 4,499 ÷ 93 _____   13. 33,617 ÷ 59 _____

14. $1,178 ÷ 33 _____   15. 712,540 ÷ 86 _____

16. Which quotient is greater: 54,689 ÷ 63 or 54,689 ÷ 59?

_____

(Mixed Review) Find each product.

17.	18.	19.	20.
517 × 39	803 × 439	347 × 99	997 × 62

Dividing by 2-Digit Divisors

Complete.

1. $16\overline{)74}$ 4 R_____

2. $29\overline{)205}$ 7 R_____

3. $42\overline{)396}$ 9 R_____

4. $33\overline{)166}$ 5 R_____

5. $78\overline{)686}$ 8 R_____

6. $61\overline{)377}$ 6 R_____

Divide.

7. $54\overline{)175}$

8. $96\overline{)488}$

9. $13\overline{)117}$

10. $25\overline{)167}$

11. $82\overline{)351}$

12. $47\overline{)401}$

13. $77\overline{)309}$

14. $50\overline{)400}$

15. $69\overline{)503}$

16. $70\overline{)150}$

17. $36\overline{)323}$

18. $28\overline{)175}$

19. $174 \div 8 =$ _____

20. $424 \div 61 =$ _____

21. $527 \div 98 =$ _____

22. $215 \div 35 =$ _____

23. What is 189 divided by 44? _____

24. Divide 166 by 20. _____

25. Can a divisor be less than a remainder? Explain.

_____

_____

_____

Dividing Greater Numbers

Divide. Check your answer.

1. $17\overline{)85}$

2. $36\overline{)288}$

3. $52\overline{)1,300}$

4. $68\overline{)1,090}$

5. $75\overline{)4,575}$

6. $43\overline{)516}$

7. $29\overline{)2,233}$

8. $84\overline{)924}$

9. $37\overline{)851}$

10. $98 \div 14 =$ _____

11. $704 \div 44 =$ _____

12. $1,801 \div 56 =$ _____

13. $2,059 \div 71 =$ _____

14. $621 \div 27$ _____

15. $376 \div 34 =$ _____

Estimate. Use your number sense to choose the best answer for **16–18.**

16. $512 \div 30$ is _____

   A. less than 17   **B.** more than 17   **C.** exactly 17

17. $1,180 \div 60$ is _____

   A. less than 2   **B.** less than 20   **C.** more than 20

18. $8,999 \div 50$ is _____

   A. less than 150   **B.** more than 200   **C.** between 150 and 200

19. Divide 686 by 26. _____

20. 735 divided by 49 is what number? _____

21. If your divisor is 63, what is the
   greatest possible remainder you could have? _____

Dividing: Choosing a Calculation Method

Divide and check. Tell what calculation method you used and why.

1. 30)‾90‾ **2.** 14)‾210‾ **3.** 40)‾165‾

4. 10)‾1,000‾ **5.** 17)‾51,000‾ **6.** 70)‾490‾

7. 62)‾7,626‾ **8.** 37)‾238‾ **9.** 60)‾360‾

10. 35)‾2,474‾ **11.** 60)‾256‾ **12.** 50)‾350‾

13. 70)‾49,000‾ **14.** 18)‾288‾ **15.** 20)‾180‾

16. 27)‾765‾ **17.** 16)‾256‾ **18.** 50)‾250‾

19. 36)‾843‾ **20.** 26)‾832‾ **21.** 24)‾888‾

22. 80)‾640‾ **23.** 38)‾342‾ **24.** 71)‾614‾

25. 4)‾320‾ **26.** 15)‾264‾ **27.** 21)‾861‾

28. 720 ÷ 90 = _____ **29.** 8,889 ÷ 29 = _____

30. 32,000 ÷ 80 = _____ **31.** 36,045 ÷ 60 = _____

Zeros in the Quotient

Divide and check.

1. 18$\overline{)735}$

2. 48$\overline{)30,256}$

3. 15$\overline{)1,063}$

4. 36$\overline{)28,980}$

5. 22$\overline{)4,565}$

6. 82$\overline{)62,324}$

7. 25$\overline{)7,642}$

8. 63$\overline{)30,902}$

9. 46$\overline{)9,649}$

10. 92$\overline{)10,120}$

11. 75$\overline{)17,313}$

12. 44$\overline{)26,547}$

13. 41,883 ÷ 82 = _____

14. 11,780 ÷ 29 = _____

15. 16,585 ÷ 54 = _____

16. 9,377 ÷ 18 = _____

17. 15,417 ÷ 28 = _____

18. 16,192 ÷ 23 = _____

Use number sense to decide whether each answer is reasonable.

19. 56$\overline{)39,312}^{\,702}$

20. 35$\overline{)17,675}^{\,42}$

21. 34$\overline{)14,280}^{\,410}$

_____   _____   _____

Exploring Algebra: Using Expressions

Decide what operation is needed; then replace the variable
with a number and do the computation.

1. There are 12 space meals in a box. How many space
meals are in n boxes?

Evaluate $12 \times n$.

a. For $n = 5$.　　　　　　　　　**b.** For $n = 12$.

$12 \times n = 12 \times$ _____　　　　$12 \times n = 12 \times$ _____

= _____ space meals　　　　= _____ space meals

Evaluate each expression for $n = 6$ and $n = 15$.

2. $n + 15$　　　　**3.** $5 \times n$　　　　**4.** $n \div 3$　　　　**5.** $n - 5$

_____ _____　　　_____ _____　　　_____ _____　　　_____ _____

6. $207 + n$　　　**7.** $10 \times n$　　　**8.** $36 - n$　　　**9.** $30 \div n$

_____ _____　　　_____ _____　　　_____ _____　　　_____ _____

Complete.

10.

n	$n + 9$
6	
15	
23	

11.

n	$n \div 4$
8	
16	
20	

12.

n	$n - 15$
30	
25	
48	

13.

n	$n \times 9$
3	
7	
9	

14. If $n = 8$, what is $7 \times n$? _____

15. If $n = 64$, what is $n \div 8$? _____

16. A baker uses 3 cups of wheat flour and n cups of rye flour in the
bread. Write an expression for the total number of cups used.

_____

Analyzing Strategies:
Use Objects/Act It Out

Use objects to solve each problem.

1. You want to design a small hotel in the shape of a cube. Each side of the hotel will be four rooms long. Use cubes to make a model.

   a. How many rooms will be on the first floor? _____

   b. How many floors high will the hotel be? _____

   c. How many rooms will be in the hotel in all? _____

   d. If you use the design, how
   many rooms will have no windows? _____

Use any strategy to solve each problem.

2. In the hotel you designed in the shape of a cube, each outside wall in each room has one window. How many rooms have a total of

   a. only one window? _____

   b. two windows? _____

3. You want to design a hotel with 24 rooms so that each room has a window on each of two walls.

   a. How many rooms will be on each floor? _____

   b. How many floors will the hotel have? _____

   c. How many windows are needed for the hotel? _____

4. You want to build a fence in the shape of a square
   around the hotel. Each side of the square has
   12 posts. There are posts on each corner of
   the square. How many posts will be needed in all? _____

5. Mr. Munez used 4.5 gallons of paint to paint each room in the hotel. The hotel has 8 floors and each floor has 9 rooms. How many gallons of paint did Mr. Munez use to paint all of the rooms in the hotel?

   _____

6. A hotel has 36 one-bed rooms, 42 two-bed rooms,
   and 12 suites. How many rooms are there in the hotel? _____

© Scott Foresman Addison Wesley 5

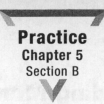
Review and Practice

(Lessons 4 and 5) Divide.

1. 32)‾155‾

2. 92)‾472‾

3. 47)‾787‾

4. 64)‾13,322‾

5. 38)‾15,599‾

6. 99)‾3,970‾

(Lesson 6) Divide and check. Tell which method you used.

7. 30)‾90,600‾

8. 15)‾3,847‾

method:

_____

method:

_____

(Lesson 7) Divide and check.

9. 3,621 ÷ 34 = _____

10. 45,127 ÷ 43 = _____

(Lesson 9) Solve.

11. 26 fifth graders collected 500 canned goods. If some students collected one more can than the rest, how many collected 19 and how many collected 20?

_____

(Mixed Review) Find each quotient.

12. 4,800 ÷ 60 = _____

13. 6,300 ÷ 700 = _____

Dividing Money

Divide and check.

1. 25)$12.50   **2.** 18)$7.92   **3.** 13)$8.97

4. 15)$24.00   **5.** 23)$32.43   **6.** 40)$246.00

7. $537.60 ÷ 35 = _____   **8.** $35.25 ÷ 75 = _____

Use your number sense to select the best answer.

9. $2.20 ÷ 40 is _____

   a. less than $0.05   **b.** more than $0.05

10. $325 ÷ 50 is _____

   a. more than $7.00   **b.** between $6.00 and $7.00

Estimate to decide whether each quotient in **11–13** is more
or less than $1.00.

11. 32)$45.00   **12.** 32)$31.00   **13.** 7)$8.08

_____   _____   _____

14. Find the quotient of $412.80 ÷ 40 = _____

15. If you had $325.50 to share with 25
people, how much should each person get? _____

Decision Making

Rock & Roll Hall of Fame and Museum
Cleveland, Ohio
Admission: $12.95 Adults, $9.50 Children
Hours: 10:00 A.M. to 5:30 P.M.

Features
Ground Level Artists' Careers Interactive Videos Mystery Train Cinema
Level 2 Memphis Recording Studio
Level 3 Museum Café
Level 4 Rock & Roll Cinema
Level 5 Radio Studio Past Hall of Fame Inductees
Level 6 Hall of Fame

1. You want to plan a day for you and your family at the Rock & Roll Hall of Fame. You buy 2 adult and 2 children admissions.

   How much do you spend? _____

2. Your family will drive 2 hours to the museum. You want to arrive at 10:00 A.M.

   What time should you leave? _____

3. You plan to spend 3 hours at the museum.

   At what time will you leave? _____

4. On which level will you eat lunch? _____

5. Name 3 levels you want to visit. _____

   _____

6. Plan a schedule. Include rest periods, gift shop, and lunch in your schedule.

Time	Activity	Time	Activity
_____	Leave home	_____	_____
_____	Arrive museum	_____	_____
_____	_____	_____	_____
_____	_____	_____	_____
_____	_____	_____	_____
_____	_____	_____	Leave museum
_____	_____	_____	Arrive home

Exploring Decimal Patterns in Division

Complete the table.

	÷	10	100	1,000
1.	1,346.5			
2.	596.3			
3.	876.42			
4.	66.75			
5.	2,002.2			

Find each quotient. Use mental math.

6. 302.6 ÷ 10 = _____   **7.** 78.61 ÷ 100 = _____

8. 362 ÷ 1,000 = _____   **9.** 13.4 ÷ 100 = _____

10. 378 ÷ 1,000 = _____   **11.** 6.25 ÷ 100 = _____

12. $925 ÷ 10 = _____   **13.** 8.49 ÷ 100 = _____

14. 4.3 ÷ 1,000 = _____   **15.** 32.25 ÷ 10 = _____

16. 823 ÷ 1,000 = _____   **17.** 73 ÷ 1,000 = _____

Use 10, 100, or 1,000 to complete each.

18. 32.7 ÷ _____ = 3.27   **19.** 632.7 ÷ _____ = 6.327

20. 435 ÷ _____ = 4.35   **21.** $85 ÷ _____ = $0.85

22. 78 ÷ _____ = 0.078   **23.** 0.26 ÷ _____ = 0.00026

Choose the word or number to complete **24–25**.

24. If you divide 3.67 by 1,000, 0 is in the _____ and hundredths places in the quotient.

25. Dividing 81.7 by 10 gives the same quotient as dividing _____ by 1,000.

26. If you were to divide 58.3 by 1,000, how many places would you move the decimal point? Explain.

Review and Practice

(Lesson 10) Find each quotient.

1. 30)$316.20

2. 17)$15.98

3. 54)$68.58

4. 22)$73.26

5. 86)$7.74

6. 40)$88.40

(Lesson 11) Use any strategy to solve each problem.

7. Would it be cheaper per ounce to buy a 20-ounce bottle
of soda for $1.35 or a 64-ounce bottle for $5.00?

_____

8. The bus for your field trip is arriving at 8:00 A.M. It is a half-hour trip to
the glass factory. There are three tours available for the class. Tour A
lasts 2 hours; tour B lasts 1 hour 45 minutes; and tour C lasts 75
minutes. If you must be back at school by noon which tours could
your class take?

_____

(Lesson 12) Find each quotient. Use mental math.

9. 54.16 ÷ 10 = _____

10. 1,245 ÷ 100 = _____

11. 4.1 ÷ 10 = _____

12. 3,745.9 ÷ 1,000 = _____

13. 0.37 ÷ 100 = _____

14. 0.2 ÷ 1,000 = _____

(Mixed Review) Subtract.

15.   4 5.6 7
        −   2.4 5

16.   3 9.0 0
        − 1 6.8

17.   5 5
        −   2.8 9

18.   7.1
        − 5.8

Cumulative Review

(Chapter 2 Lesson 19) Choose an operation then solve.

1. Rob is 60 inches tall. He has grown 7 inches in the last 5 years. How tall was he 5 years ago? _____

(Chapter 3 Lesson 16) Solve.

2. At the scout shop a compass costs $5 and a flashlight costs $8. The scouts spent a total of $90 on 15 items. How many compasses and how many flashlights did they buy?

_____

(Chapter 4 Lesson 15) Solve.

3. If you add 3 to Sandro's age and divide by 3 you get 6. How old is Sandro? _____

(Chapter 4 Lesson 12) Find each quotient.

4. $3\overline{)29.202}$ 5. $5\overline{)8.275}$ 6. $6\overline{)67.224}$

(Chapter 5 Lessons 4 and 10) Divide.

7. $23\overline{)221}$ 8. $16\overline{)133}$ 9. $48\overline{)153}$

10. $21\overline{)\$99.96}$ 11. $13\overline{)\$8.97}$ 12. $40\overline{)\$675.20}$

Lines and Angles

Write the name for each.

1. _____

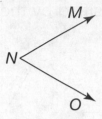

2. _____

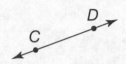

3. _____

4. _____

5. _____

6. _____

Name each in the figure at the right.

7. the rays that form ∠ T

_____

8. the angle that has R as its vertex

_____

9. perpendicular lines

_____

10. parallel lines

_____

11. the rays that form ∠U

_____

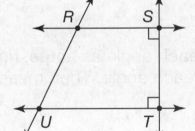

Exploring Measuring Angles

1. Angles can be classified by the way their measures compare to 90°.

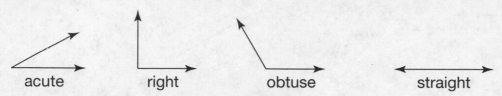

acute   right   obtuse   straight

a. Which angle measure is 90°? _____

b. Which angle measure is greater than 90° and less than 180°? _____

c. Which angle measure is less than 90°? _____

d. Which angle measures 180°? _____

2. Extend the sides of each angle. Use a protractor to measure each angle.

a. _____   **b.** _____

Identify each angle as acute, right, or obtuse. Extend the sides of each angle. Then measure each with a protractor.

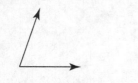   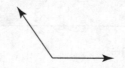

3. _____   **4.** _____

5. _____   **6.** _____

Triangles

1. Classify each triangle as equilateral, isosceles,
or scalene.

 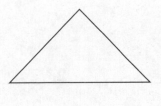 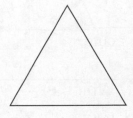

a. _____ **b.** _____ **c.** _____

2. Classify each triangle as acute, right, or obtuse.

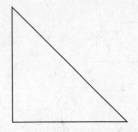 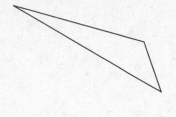 

a. _____ **b.** _____ **c.** _____

3. Evan drew a triangle with a 100°
angle. Could it be acute, right, or obtuse? _____

4. Rachel drew a triangle with a 90° angle. Were
the other angles acute, obtuse or right? _____

5. Tanisha drew a triangle with a 45° angle.
Could it be acute, right, or obtuse? _____

6. Draw a right, an acute and an obtuse triangle. Write
whether each is scalene, isosceles or equilateral.

a. **b.** **c.**

_____ _____ _____

Quadrilaterals

Write the name that best describes each figure.

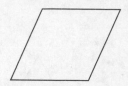

1. _____

2. _____

3. _____

4. _____

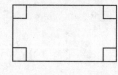

5. _____

6. _____

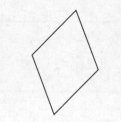

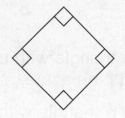

7. _____

8. _____

9. Ivan is making a design using a quadrilateral that has two pairs of parallel sides with all sides the same length, but with no right angles. What shape is he using? _____

10. You are making a design using a quadrilateral with only one pair of parallel sides. What shape could you use? _____

Analyze Strategies: Solve a Simpler Problem

1. Karen rides her bike to school every day. How many different routes can Karen take to get to school without backtracking?

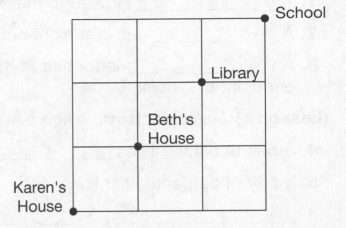

a. How many different routes can Karen take to get to Beth's house?

_____

b. How many different routes can Karen take to get to the library?

_____

c. How many different routes can Karen take to get to school? _____

2. If you cut a piece of clay with 3 intersecting lines, you can get 7 pieces of clay. What is the greatest number of pieces you can get by cutting the clay with 5 intersecting lines? _____

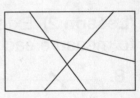

Use any strategy to solve each problem.

3. If 14 students are playing musical chairs, how many times does the music have to stop for someone to win the game if one chair is removed at a time? _____

4. You're playing in a baseball tournament with 8 teams. Each team plays until they lose. What is the most number of games one team will play? _____

5. The Rockets beat the Tigers in a game of baseball. The Rockets scored 4 more runs than the Tigers. The total number of runs scored was 14. What was the score? _____

Name _____

Review and Practice

Vocabulary Complete with the correct word from the list.

1. A _____ is used to measure angles.

2. A _____ is a straight path that goes on forever.

3. An _____ is formed at the shared endpoint of 2 rays.

protractor
line
angle

(Lesson 1) Name each in the figure at the right.

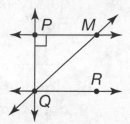

4. a pair of parallel lines _____

5. a pair of perpendicular lines

_____

6. a pair of intersecting lines

_____

7. the rays that form angle *M* _____

(Lesson 2) Extend the lines of each angle. Use a protractor to measure each angle.

8. _____

9. 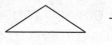 _____

(Lesson 3) Classify each triangle as equilateral, isosceles, or scalene. Then classify each triangle as acute, right, or obtuse.

10. _____,

_____

11.  _____,

_____

(Lesson 4) Write the name that best describes each figure.

12.

13.

14.

_____   _____   _____

(Mixed Review) Find each product.

15. $50 \times 70 =$ _____

16. $46 \times 3 =$ _____

17. $8 \times 3,000 =$ _____

18. $70 \times 900 =$ _____

Similar and Congruent Polygons

Circle the polygon similar to the first one in each row.

1.   **a.**   **b.**   **c.**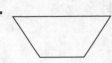

2.   **a.** 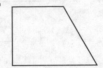 **b.**   **c.**

3.   **a.**   **b.**   **c.**

Circle the polygon congruent to the first one in each row.

4.   **a.**   **b.**   **c.**

5.   **a.**   **b.**   **c.**

6.   **a.**   **b.**   **c.**

7. Are two congruent figures similar?

_____

_____

Name _____

Exploring Congruence and Motions

Write the motion used to get from start to finish.

1. _____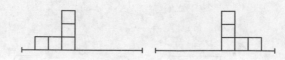

2. _____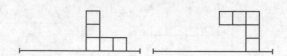

3. _____

4. For each pentomino pair, write whether you would flip, turn, or slide the figures to show that they are congruent.

   a.

   b.

   _____   _____

5. Which of the figures is congruent to ? _____

   a.    b.   c.   d.

6. Which of the figures is **not** congruent to ? _____

   a.   b.   c.   d.

7. Which of the figures shows turned? _____

   a.   b.   c.   d.

Exploring Line Symmetry

1. Explain how tracing a figure can help you find its lines of symmetry.

_____

_____

_____

Draw all lines of symmetry.

2.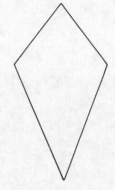

3.

Use the line of symmetry to complete each figure.

4.

5.

Use flips, turns, or slides. Is each pair of figures congruent? Explain.

6.

7.

_____   _____

8. Draw three hexominoes that have at least 1 line of symmetry.

Decision Making

You want to complete an art project over the weekend. You have to decide between 2 project choices. You will be working by yourself. Here are the 2 project choices:

Polygon Collage: Make a collage by drawing, cutting out, and pasting polygons. Include some similar and congruent figures.

Mask: Make a mask that is symmetrical. It should have 1 line of symmetry.

In order to decide which project to complete, you need to think about some details of the project. Answer the following questions:

1. How much time do you
   have to work on the project? _____

2. Do you have the materials
   you need for each project? _____

3. Will you be able to use either of the projects in
   the future?

   Polygon Collage: _____   Mask: _____

4. Which project would
   you enjoy completing? _____

5. Write an estimate of how much time each project will take.

   Polygon Collage: _____

   Mask: _____

6. Divide the time you will need for each project equally
   among the number of days in the weekend.

   Polygon Collage: _____ each day   Mask: _____ each day

7. Think about your answers to the questions above. Which
   project would you choose to complete? Why?

   _____

   _____

© Scott Foresman Addison Wesley 5

Review and Practice

Vocabulary Match each with its definition.

_____ **1.** congruent polygons

_____ **2.** pentominoes

_____ **3.** similar figures

_____ **4.** line of symmetry

a. have the same shape, but not necessarily same size

b. have the same shape and size

c. five congruent squares joined

d. separates a shape into two congruent halves

(Lesson 6) Use the figures to answer **5** and **6**.

  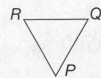 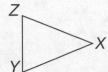

5. Which triangle is congruent to triangle *ABC*? _____

6. Which triangle is similar to triangle *XYZ*? _____

(Lesson 7) Use the figures to answer **7** and **8**.

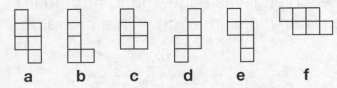

7. Which figures are pentominoes? _____

8. Which figures are congruent? _____

(Lesson 8) Draw all lines of symmetry.

9.

10.

(Mixed Review) Add or subtract.

11.	**12.**	**13.**	**14.**
3,248	5,733	1,911	3,067
+ 2,638	− 2,885	− 992	+ 7,864

Name _____

Cumulative Review

(Chapter 4 Lesson 13)

1. Which numbers in **2–7** are divisible by 3? _____

(Chapter 4 Lesson 14) Write prime or composite for each number.

2. 26 _____   **3.** 111 _____   **4.** 31 _____

5. 47 _____   **6.** 61 _____   **7.** 57 _____

(Chapter 5 Lessons 4 and 5) Divide.

8. $42\overline{)369}$ **9.** $85\overline{)710}$ **10.** $55\overline{)493}$

11. $34\overline{)642}$ **12.** $26\overline{)478}$ **13.** $58\overline{)944}$

(Chapter 6 Lesson 2) Identify each angle as acute, right, or obtuse. Extend the sides of each angle. Then measure each with a protractor.

14.   **15.**   **16.**

_____   _____   _____

(Chapter 6 Lesson 6) Use the figure to answer **17–20.**

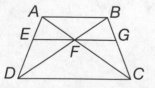

17. Name a triangle congruent to triangle *AFD.* _____

18. Name a triangle similar to triangle *CDF.* _____

19. Name a triangle congruent to triangle *ABD.* _____

20. Name a trapezoid similar to trapezoid *GFDC.* _____

Whole and Parts

Write the fraction that names each shaded part.

1.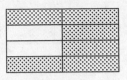

2.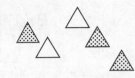

_____

_____

What part of each set is square?

3.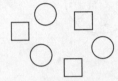

4.

_____

_____

5. Which shows three fourths? _____

A.

B.

6. Estimate the fraction of
the figure that is shaded. _____

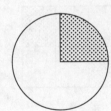

A. $\frac{1}{8}$ **B.** $\frac{1}{4}$ **C.** $\frac{1}{2}$

7. During an art contest at your school, you and a
classmate each won blue ribbons for $\frac{1}{3}$ of the pieces
you entered in the contest. You won 2 blue ribbons
and your classmate won 3 blue ribbons. Explain how
this could be.

_____

_____

Name _____

Exploring Equivalent Fractions

1. Which shadings show fractions equivalent to $\frac{2}{3}$? _____

   A.   B. 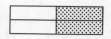   C.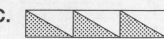

Write two fractions that name the shaded part.

2.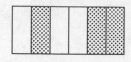

3.

4.

_____   _____   _____

5. Write a fraction for the shaded part of
   each picture. Which fractions are equivalent to $\frac{1}{3}$?

   A.

   B.

   _____   _____

   C.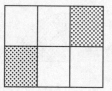

   D.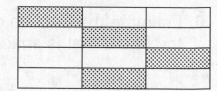

   _____   _____

   Fractions _____ are all equivalent to $\frac{1}{3}$.

6. John's mother baked a lasagna in a rectangular pan and cut it into 6
   pieces. John ate 2 pieces.

   a. Draw a picture to represent
      the lasagna and shade in
      the pieces that John ate.

   b. Write 2 fractions that describe how much lasagna is left. _____

7. Gina said she would share half a pack of baseball cards with Joe.
   Joe ended up with $\frac{5}{10}$ of the pack. Did Joe get half? Explain.

_____

Patterns with Equivalent Fractions

Find equivalent fractions with a denominator of 8.

1. $\frac{1}{2}$

2. $\frac{3}{4}$

3. $\frac{9}{24}$

4. $\frac{25}{40}$

_____   _____   _____   _____

Find equivalent fractions with a denominator of 12.

5. $\frac{2}{3}$

6. $\frac{5}{6}$

7. $\frac{8}{24}$

8. $\frac{9}{36}$

_____   _____   _____   _____

Name the fractions in the box equivalent to each fraction below.

$$\boxed{\frac{12}{16} \quad \frac{3}{6} \quad \frac{9}{12} \quad \frac{2}{4} \quad \frac{3}{9} \quad \frac{6}{8} \quad \frac{4}{8} \quad \frac{2}{6} \quad \frac{4}{12}}$$

9. $\frac{1}{3}$

10. $\frac{3}{4}$

11. $\frac{1}{2}$

12. $\frac{2}{6}$

_____   _____   _____   _____

Write whether each pair is equivalent. Explain how you decided.

13. $\frac{1}{4}$ and $\frac{3}{12}$

_____

14. $\frac{12}{18}$ and $\frac{3}{9}$

_____

15. $\frac{4}{5}$ and $\frac{12}{15}$

_____

16. Three-ninths of a soccer game is over. Is this half-time?
Explain.

_____

Greatest Common Factor

Find the greatest common factor for each pair.

1. 4 and 8   **2.** 6 and 9   **3.** 12 and 18   **4.** 10 and 15

_____   _____   _____   _____

5. 6 and 12   **6.** 14 and 21   **7.** 6 and 18   **8.** 16 and 24

_____   _____   _____   _____

9. 6 and 15   **10.** 4 and 10   **11.** 3 and 7   **12.** 9 and 15

_____   _____   _____   _____

13. 5 and 12   **14.** 7 and 4   **15.** 2 and 5   **16.** 12 and 9

_____   _____   _____   _____

17. Find two numbers that have 6 as the greatest common factor.

_____

18. Find two numbers that have 10 as the greatest common factor.

_____

19. Find the factors of 12 and 16.   **20.** Find the factors of 8 and 20

_____   _____

_____   _____

21. Could 7 be the greatest common factor of 21 and 35?
Explain.

_____

22. The common factors of two numbers are 2 and 4.
The two numbers could be 12 and 16 or 8 and 24.
Explain how.

_____

_____

Simplest Form

Find the simplest form for each fraction.

1. $\frac{12}{16}$ **2.** $\frac{8}{24}$ **3.** $\frac{3}{9}$ **4.** $\frac{8}{16}$ **5.** $\frac{10}{15}$

_____   _____   _____   _____   _____

6. $\frac{14}{21}$ **7.** $\frac{12}{18}$ **8.** $\frac{9}{27}$ **9.** $\frac{6}{9}$ **10.** $\frac{8}{10}$

_____   _____   _____   _____   _____

11. $\frac{7}{21}$ **12.** $\frac{5}{15}$ **13.** $\frac{12}{15}$ **14.** $\frac{12}{16}$ **15.** $\frac{15}{18}$

_____   _____   _____   _____   _____

16. $\frac{5}{25}$ **17.** $\frac{12}{18}$ **18.** $\frac{16}{20}$ **19.** $\frac{6}{20}$ **20.** $\frac{8}{48}$

_____   _____   _____   _____   _____

21. $\frac{6}{48}$ **22.** $\frac{32}{40}$ **23.** $\frac{35}{42}$ **24.** $\frac{9}{45}$ **25.** $\frac{18}{27}$

_____   _____   _____   _____   _____

Write whether each fraction is in simplest form. If it is not, find the simplest form.

26. $\frac{2}{6}$ **27.** $\frac{3}{15}$ **28.** $\frac{5}{6}$ **29.** $\frac{9}{12}$ **30.** $\frac{1}{3}$

_____   _____   _____   _____   _____

31. $\frac{2}{7}$ **32.** $\frac{6}{10}$ **33.** $\frac{7}{8}$ **34.** $\frac{6}{8}$ **35.** $\frac{5}{35}$

_____   _____   _____   _____   _____

36. Explain why a fraction whose denominator is 13 is always in its simplest form.

_____

Exploring Comparing and Ordering Fractions

1. Describe how you compare two fractions whose numerators are the same.

_____

_____

Compare each pair of fractions. You may use fraction strips or draw pictures. Write >, < or = to complete.

2. $\frac{1}{4} \bigcirc \frac{1}{5}$ **3.** $\frac{3}{4} \bigcirc \frac{1}{4}$ **4.** $\frac{4}{7} \bigcirc \frac{4}{5}$

5. $\frac{3}{7} \bigcirc \frac{3}{9}$ **6.** $\frac{2}{7} \bigcirc \frac{4}{7}$ **7.** $\frac{1}{3} \bigcirc \frac{1}{6}$

8. $\frac{5}{8} \bigcirc \frac{8}{8}$ **9.** $\frac{2}{3} \bigcirc \frac{2}{5}$ **10.** $\frac{1}{8} \bigcirc \frac{1}{3}$

11. $\frac{1}{2} \bigcirc \frac{5}{8}$ **12.** $\frac{2}{3} \bigcirc \frac{10}{15}$ **13.** $\frac{2}{3} \bigcirc \frac{6}{7}$

14. $\frac{3}{8} \bigcirc \frac{3}{7}$ **15.** $\frac{6}{7} \bigcirc \frac{5}{7}$ **16.** $\frac{1}{6} \bigcirc \frac{1}{8}$

Order these fractions from least to greatest. Use fraction strips.

17. $\frac{3}{8}, \frac{2}{3}, \frac{4}{5}$ _____, _____, _____

18. $\frac{8}{9}, \frac{11}{12}, \frac{10}{11}$ _____, _____, _____

19. Is $\frac{1}{4}$ greater than or less than $\frac{1}{8}$? Explain.

_____

_____

20. Peter ate $\frac{2}{3}$ of a pizza. Jordan ate $\frac{4}{8}$ of a same size pizza.

Who ate more? _____

Name _____

Comparing and Ordering Fractions

Write >, < or = to complete.

1. $\frac{1}{2} \bigcirc \frac{1}{3}$ **2.** $\frac{1}{2} \bigcirc \frac{2}{3}$ **3.** $\frac{1}{4} \bigcirc \frac{1}{3}$

4. $\frac{1}{4} \bigcirc \frac{1}{6}$ **5.** $\frac{1}{3} \bigcirc \frac{1}{5}$ **6.** $\frac{2}{5} \bigcirc \frac{1}{3}$

7. $\frac{2}{5} \bigcirc \frac{2}{3}$ **8.** $\frac{8}{12} \bigcirc \frac{2}{3}$ **9.** $\frac{2}{3} \bigcirc \frac{4}{5}$

10. $\frac{5}{8} \bigcirc \frac{1}{2}$ **11.** $\frac{1}{2} \bigcirc \frac{3}{8}$ **12.** $\frac{4}{10} \bigcirc \frac{6}{15}$

13. $\frac{7}{10} \bigcirc \frac{3}{4}$ **14.** $\frac{7}{10} \bigcirc \frac{2}{3}$ **15.** $\frac{5}{6} \bigcirc \frac{7}{12}$

16. $\frac{3}{10} \bigcirc \frac{7}{10}$ **17.** $\frac{1}{4} \bigcirc \frac{3}{10}$ **18.** $\frac{1}{6} \bigcirc \frac{1}{10}$

Compare the fractions. Write them in order from least to greatest.

19. $\frac{1}{2}, \frac{1}{3}, \frac{1}{4}$, _____

20. $\frac{2}{3}, \frac{13}{18}, \frac{7}{9}, \frac{5}{6}$, _____

21. $\frac{3}{4}, \frac{3}{8}, \frac{3}{7}$, _____

22. $\frac{3}{5}, \frac{1}{2}, \frac{1}{4}, \frac{2}{5}$, _____

23. Explain how four red marbles can make up $\frac{1}{3}$ of a group of marbles and three blue marbles make up $\frac{1}{4}$ of the same group.

_____

_____

24. Joe has $\frac{1}{6}$ of a packet of crackers and Aaron has $\frac{3}{8}$. Who has more crackers?

_____

Analyze Strategies: Make a Table

Make a table or use another strategy to solve each problem.

1. For every 10 videos Video Palace rents, 5 are comedy videos. If they rent 30 videos, how many are comedy videos?

_____

2. For every 2 hours Karen does yard work, her brother, Jeff works 4 hours cleaning the house. If Jeff works in the house for 12 hours a month, how many hours would Karen work on the yard?

_____

3. José used his new telescope to view the stars. On his first night he observed 7 stars. Every night that followed he discovered 3 new stars he hadn't seen before. On the fifth night how many stars did José observe altogether?

_____

4. The local ice cream shop was selling 20 shakes in a day. Then they advertised a special on their shakes, and their sales doubled every day. On the fourth day of the advertisement, how many shakes did they sell?

_____

5. Mrs. Gupta came home from the mall with $14. At her last stop before coming home she bought some paint and paint brushes at an art supply store for $9.50. Earlier she had purchased some overalls for $23.50. How much money did Mrs Gupta take with her to the mall?

_____

6. Lana drives 6 miles every day, and Fred drives 7 miles every day. If Fred has driven 56 miles, how many miles has Lana driven?

_____

Review and Practice

Vocabulary Write true or false for each statement.

1. The denominator is the bottom number in a fraction. _____

2. A fraction is in simplest form when the GCF
   of the numerator and denominator is less than 3. _____

3. $\frac{2}{3}$ and $\frac{3}{4}$ are equivalent fractions. _____

(Lesson 1) Write the fraction that names each shaded part.

4. _____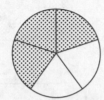

5. _____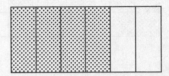

(Lessons 2 and 3) Complete.

6. $\frac{3}{4} = \frac{\square}{12} = \frac{6}{\square} = \frac{\square}{16}$

7. $\frac{5}{6} = \frac{10}{\square} = \frac{\square}{60}$

(Lesson 4) Find the greatest comon factor for each pair.

8. 12 and 8 _____

9. 20 and 9 _____

(Lesson 5) Find the simplest form for each fraction.

10. $\frac{22}{66} =$ _____

11. $\frac{36}{48} =$ _____

12. $\frac{14}{16} =$ _____

(Lessons 6 and 7) Write each set of fractions in order from least to greatest.

13. $\frac{1}{6}, \frac{2}{3}, \frac{1}{5}$ _____,_____,_____

14. $\frac{5}{6}, \frac{9}{12}, \frac{5}{8}$ _____,_____,_____

(Lesson 8) Solve. You may make a table to help.

15. On Monday, Megan found a 3-leaf plant. On Tuesday, she
    found a 4-leaf plant and on Wednesday she found a 5-leaf
    plant. If she continues to find plants in the same pattern,
    on what day of the week would she find a 10-leaf plant?

    _____

(Mixed Review) Complete each number sentence.

16. 36 ÷ _____ = 4   17. _____ ÷ 6 = 8   18. _____ × 7 = 56

Exploring Mixed Numbers

Match each with its definition.

_____ **1.** mixed number

_____ **2.** improper fraction

a. a whole number and a fraction

b. a fraction greater than, or equal to, 1

Write the mixed or whole number and the improper fraction that name each shaded part.

3.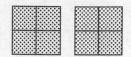

4.

_____

_____

5.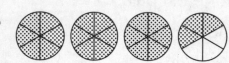

6.

_____

_____

7.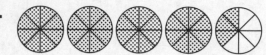

8.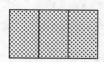

_____

_____

9.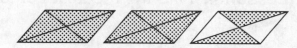

10.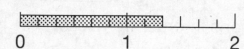

_____

_____

Make a drawing that shows each fraction.

11. $2\frac{3}{5}$

12. $\frac{15}{3}$

13. $2\frac{2}{3}$

14. $\frac{7}{2}$

Mixed Numbers

Write each improper fraction as a mixed number in simplest form, or as a whole number.

1. $\frac{11}{3} =$ _____

2. $\frac{19}{5} =$ _____

3. $\frac{25}{3} =$ _____

4. $\frac{42}{6} =$ _____

5. $\frac{43}{8} =$ _____

6. $\frac{49}{6} =$ _____

7. $\frac{36}{4} =$ _____

8. $\frac{68}{9} =$ _____

9. $\frac{23}{4} =$ _____

10. $\frac{96}{8} =$ _____

11. $\frac{23}{5} =$ _____

12. $\frac{34}{3} =$ _____

13. $\frac{72}{5} =$ _____

14. $\frac{46}{6} =$ _____

15. $\frac{49}{7} =$ _____

Write each mixed number as an improper fraction.

16. $3\frac{1}{2} =$ _____

17. $5\frac{3}{4} =$ _____

18. $6\frac{7}{8} =$ _____

19. $5\frac{5}{12} =$ _____

20. $4\frac{1}{6} =$ _____

21. $6\frac{2}{3} =$ _____

22. $12\frac{2}{3} =$ _____

23. $9\frac{1}{4} =$ _____

24. $8\frac{2}{5} =$ _____

25. $25\frac{1}{4} =$ _____

26. $22\frac{1}{2} =$ _____

27. $6\frac{4}{5} =$ _____

28. $11\frac{3}{8} =$ _____

29. $16\frac{5}{6} =$ _____

30. $9\frac{8}{9} =$ _____

Complete.

31. $2 = \frac{\square}{20}$

32. $6 = \frac{\square}{3}$

33. $8 = \frac{\square}{5}$

34. $7\frac{1}{2} = \frac{\square}{6}$

35. $4\frac{3}{5} = \frac{\square}{5}$

36. $11\frac{1}{2} = \frac{\square}{2}$

37. The pizza at Ryan's party is divided into eighths. Ryan usually eats 3 slices and the rest of his family usually eats 13. Are 2 pizzas enough? Explain.

_____

_____

Exploring Comparing and Ordering Mixed Numbers

1. How do you know $2\frac{1}{3}$ is greater than $1\frac{5}{6}$ without comparing the fractions?

_____

2. Can you just compare the whole numbers when comparing $1\frac{3}{4}$ and $1\frac{1}{3}$? Explain. _____

_____

Give a mixed number for the shaded part of each picture.
Use > and < to compare each pair of mixed numbers.

3.

_____ $\bigcirc$ _____

4.

_____ $\bigcirc$ _____

5.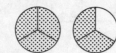

_____ $\bigcirc$ _____

Compare. Use > or <.

6. $4\frac{3}{8}$ $\bigcirc$ $5\frac{1}{6}$ **7.** $2\frac{2}{3}$ $\bigcirc$ $2\frac{1}{4}$ **8.** $3\frac{1}{8}$ $\bigcirc$ $3\frac{1}{6}$

9. $2\frac{5}{8}$ $\bigcirc$ $2\frac{3}{4}$ **10.** $6\frac{2}{3}$ $\bigcirc$ $4\frac{7}{8}$ **11.** $3\frac{7}{10}$ $\bigcirc$ $\frac{17}{4}$

Write in order from least to greatest.

12. $2\frac{1}{2}$, $\frac{9}{4}$, $\frac{8}{3}$, $1\frac{4}{5}$ _____

Name _____

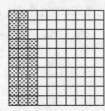
Understanding Percent

Write the fraction and the percent shaded in each picture.

1.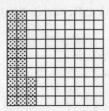

2.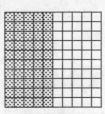

3.

_____   _____   _____

Write each as a percent.

4. 78 out of 100 _____   **5.** 83 out of 100 _____

6. 55 out of 100 _____   **7.** $\frac{25}{100}$ _____

Write each as a hundredths fraction.

8. 82% _____   **9.** 6% _____

10. 59% _____   **11.** 60% _____

For each set, decide which does **not** belong.

12. A. 32%   **B.** 32 out of 100   **C.** $\frac{3}{100}$ **D.** $\frac{32}{100}$ _____

13. A. $\frac{49}{100}$ **B.** $\frac{4}{9}$ **C.** 49 out of 100   **D.** 49% _____

Estimation Estimate the percent of each figure that is shaded.

14.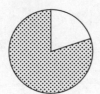

15.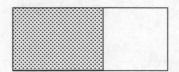

_____   _____

Name _____

Connecting Fractions, Decimals and Percents

Write a fraction, a decimal, and a percent that name each shaded part.

1.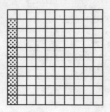

_____

_____

_____

2.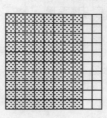

_____

_____

_____

3.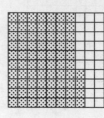

_____

_____

_____

Write each as a percent.

4. 5 out of 100

_____

5. 89 out of 100

_____

6. 0.65

_____

7. 0.09

_____

8. $\frac{4}{100}$

_____

9. $\frac{57}{100}$

_____

Write each as a fraction and a decimal.

10. 3%

_____

_____

11. 59%

_____

_____

12. 35%

_____

_____

13. 41%

_____

_____

14. 5%

_____

_____

15. 37%

_____

_____

16. Which is less: $\frac{1}{3}$ or 50%?

_____

17. Which is greater: 0.06 or 60%?

_____

Name _____

Decision Making

It's the start of football season. Suppose you read a survey of favorite teams taken at Sandburg School. You decide to survey 50 students at your own school.

Favorite Football Teams Sandburg School		Votes for Favorite Teams at Your School	
Cowboys	10%	Cowboys	5
49ers	30%	49ers	10
Steelers	25%	Steelers	20
Eagles	25%	Eagles	5
Broncos	10%	Broncos	10

1. Write fractions, decimals, and percents to describe the survey results at your school.

	Fraction	Decimal	Percent
a. Cowboys	_____	_____	_____
b. 49ers	_____	_____	_____
c. Steelers	_____	_____	_____
d. Eagles	_____	_____	_____
e. Broncos	_____	_____	_____

2. Which team is the favorite at Sandburg School? _____

3. Which team is the least favorite overall? _____

4. Which team has the biggest difference between the two surveys?

_____

5. Draw a circle graph for each survey.

Name _____

Review and Practice

Vocabulary Match each with its example.

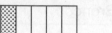 $2\frac{1}{5}$, $\frac{12}{7}$, 15%

1. percent   **2.** improper fraction   **3.** mixed number

_____   _____   _____

(Lesson 9) Write the mixed or whole number and the improper fraction that name each shaded part.

4.    **5.**

_____   _____

(Lesson 10) Write each improper fraction as a mixed number in simplest form or a whole number. Write each mixed number as an improper fraction.

6. $\frac{24}{15}$ = _____   **7.** $\frac{36}{12}$ = _____   **8.** $2\frac{4}{5}$ = _____

(Lesson 11) Write >, <, or = to complete.

9. $3\frac{2}{3}$ ◯ $1\frac{4}{5}$ **10.** $6\frac{4}{8}$ ◯ $6\frac{3}{6}$ **11.** $2\frac{6}{9}$ ◯ $2\frac{1}{5}$

(Lessons 12 and 14) Use the circle graph to answer **12** and **13**.

12. What fractional part of those surveyed favored red? _____

13. What percent favored green or blue? _____

Favorite Colors

(Mixed Review) Add or subtract.

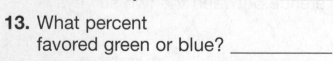

14.   6 9,2 9 4
      + 1 3,9 2 0

15.   1 8,5 1 7
      −   9,3 6 8

16.   8 0 6
      + 7 3 6

17.   9 9
      − 4 5

Cumulative Review

(Chapter 1 Lesson 6) Tell which operation you would use. Then solve.

1. There are 28 people on a hike. Each person carried a backpack weighing 5 pounds. How many pounds were carried in all?

_____

(Chapter 3 Lesson 10) Multiply.

2. $3.69	3. 37.1	4. $9.01	5. 0.159
× 3	× 8	× 6	× 7

(Chapter 6 Lesson 3) Name each triangle by its sides and angles.

6. 　　7. 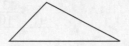　　8.

_____　_____　_____

_____　_____　_____

(Chapter 6 Lesson 8) Draw all lines of symmetry.

9. 　　10. 　　11.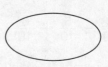

(Chapter 7 Lesson 5) Write the simplest form for each fraction.

12. $\frac{8}{16}$ = _____　　13. $\frac{12}{32}$ = _____　　14. $\frac{6}{14}$ = _____

15. $\frac{15}{35}$ = _____　　16. $\frac{20}{30}$ = _____　　17. $\frac{33}{99}$ = _____

(Chapter 7 Lesson 11) Write in order from least to greatest.

18. $2\frac{1}{4}$, $1\frac{5}{6}$, $1\frac{1}{4}$ 　　　　　　　19. $2\frac{2}{3}$, $5\frac{1}{5}$, $2\frac{1}{5}$

_____, _____, _____ 　　　　_____, _____, _____

Adding and Subtracting Fractions with Like Denominators

Find each sum or difference. Simplify.

1. $\frac{4}{6} + \frac{1}{6}$

2. $\frac{7}{8} - \frac{4}{8}$

3. $\frac{8}{10} - \frac{5}{10}$

4. $\frac{2}{3} + \frac{2}{3}$

_____

_____

_____

_____

5. $\frac{2}{6}$
$- \frac{1}{6}$

6. $\frac{7}{8}$
$+ \frac{1}{8}$

7. $\frac{6}{9}$
$- \frac{3}{9}$

8. $\frac{2}{7}$
$+ \frac{6}{7}$

9. $\frac{8}{9}$
$- \frac{5}{9}$

10. $\frac{7}{8}$
$+ \frac{3}{8}$

11. $\frac{8}{10}$
$- \frac{3}{10}$

12. $\frac{2}{12}$
$+ \frac{10}{12}$

13. $\frac{7}{8} + \frac{7}{8}$

14. $\frac{6}{10} - \frac{2}{10}$

15. $\frac{3}{9} + \frac{3}{9} + \frac{3}{9}$

_____

_____

_____

16. $\frac{2}{10} + \frac{5}{10} + \frac{6}{10}$

17. $\frac{7}{12} + \frac{3}{12} + \frac{4}{12}$

18. $\frac{2}{8} + \frac{4}{8} + \frac{6}{8}$

_____

_____

_____

19. $\frac{2}{6} + \frac{3}{6} + \frac{4}{6}$

20. $\frac{1}{2} + \frac{1}{2} + \frac{1}{2}$

21. $\frac{4}{5} + \frac{1}{5} + \frac{2}{5}$

_____

_____

_____

22. Find the sum of $\frac{8}{9}$ and $\frac{4}{9}$. _____

23. Why does $\frac{3}{9} + \frac{6}{9} = \frac{6}{9} + \frac{3}{9}$? Explain.

_____

_____

Exploring Adding Fractions

1. $\frac{1}{2} + \frac{1}{4}$

| $\frac{1}{2}$ | $\frac{1}{4}$ |

↓

| $\frac{2}{4}$ | $\frac{1}{4}$ |
| $\frac{3}{4}$ |

_____ $+ \frac{1}{4} =$ _____

Find each sum.

2. $\frac{2}{3} + \frac{1}{6}$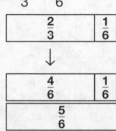

| $\frac{2}{3}$ | $\frac{1}{6}$ |

↓

| $\frac{4}{6}$ | $\frac{1}{6}$ |
| $\frac{5}{6}$ |

_____

3. $\frac{1}{2} + \frac{3}{8}$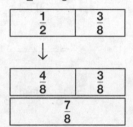

| $\frac{1}{2}$ | $\frac{3}{8}$ |

↓

| $\frac{4}{8}$ | $\frac{3}{8}$ |
| $\frac{7}{8}$ |

_____

4. $\frac{4}{9} + \frac{1}{3}$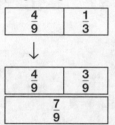

| $\frac{4}{9}$ | $\frac{1}{3}$ |

↓

| $\frac{4}{9}$ | $\frac{3}{9}$ |
| $\frac{7}{9}$ |

_____

Find each sum. You may use fraction strips or draw pictures to help.

5. $\frac{4}{5} + \frac{1}{10}$

6. $\frac{2}{3} + \frac{2}{9}$

7. $\frac{2}{5} + \frac{1}{2}$

8. $\frac{1}{3} + \frac{1}{6}$

_____   _____   _____   _____

9. $\begin{array}{r} \frac{2}{9} \\ + \frac{1}{3} \\ \hline \end{array}$

10. $\begin{array}{r} \frac{2}{3} \\ + \frac{5}{6} \\ \hline \end{array}$

11. $\begin{array}{r} \frac{2}{5} \\ + \frac{2}{3} \\ \hline \end{array}$

12. $\begin{array}{r} \frac{2}{9} \\ + \frac{1}{3} \\ \hline \end{array}$

13. $\frac{1}{8} + \frac{1}{2} + \frac{3}{4}$

14. $\frac{2}{3} + \frac{1}{3} + \frac{5}{6}$

15. $\frac{1}{2} + \frac{2}{8} + \frac{1}{4}$

_____   _____   _____

16. Find the sum of $\frac{2}{5}$ and $\frac{7}{10}$. _____

17. Find the sum of $\frac{1}{3}$ and $\frac{5}{9}$. _____

Least Common Denominator

Find the LCD for each pair of fractions.

1. $\frac{3}{5}$ and $\frac{1}{2}$

2. $\frac{2}{3}$ and $\frac{3}{5}$

3. $\frac{3}{4}$ and $\frac{3}{8}$

4. $\frac{5}{12}$ and $\frac{1}{4}$

_____

_____

_____

_____

5. $\frac{1}{3}$ and $\frac{2}{5}$

6. $\frac{1}{4}$ and $\frac{3}{10}$

7. $\frac{4}{9}$ and $\frac{5}{12}$

8. $\frac{3}{8}$ and $\frac{5}{12}$

_____

_____

_____

_____

9. $\frac{9}{12}$ and $\frac{3}{9}$

10. $\frac{3}{5}$ and $\frac{2}{7}$

11. $\frac{2}{3}$ and $\frac{1}{4}$

12. $\frac{2}{9}$ and $\frac{1}{8}$

_____

_____

_____

_____

13. $\frac{1}{6}$ and $\frac{4}{9}$

14. $\frac{1}{4}$ and $\frac{3}{9}$

15. $\frac{2}{6}$ and $\frac{1}{8}$

16. $\frac{2}{7}$ and $\frac{3}{4}$

_____

_____

_____

_____

17. Why is the LCD of $\frac{3}{4}$ and $\frac{4}{8}$ not the product of 4 and 8?

_____

18. Why is the LCD of $\frac{5}{9}$ and $\frac{7}{12}$ not the product of 9 and 12?

_____

19. If you know that the least common multiple (LCM) of 3 and 7 is 21, what do you also know about the least common denominator (LCD) of $\frac{2}{3}$ and $\frac{4}{7}$?

_____

20. If you know that the least common multiple (LCM) of 4 and 6 is 12, what do you also know about the least common denominator (LCD) of $\frac{3}{4}$ and $\frac{5}{6}$?

_____

Adding Fractions

Find each sum. Simplify.

1. $\frac{1}{4} + \frac{4}{5}$ **2.** $\frac{2}{5} + \frac{2}{3}$ **3.** $\frac{3}{8} + \frac{2}{3}$ **4.** $\frac{2}{3} + \frac{4}{5}$

_____   _____   _____   _____

5. $\frac{7}{8}$ **6.** $\frac{7}{12}$ **7.** $\frac{3}{4}$ **8.** $\frac{2}{5}$

$+ \frac{2}{3}$ $+ \frac{7}{8}$ $+ \frac{5}{12}$ $+ \frac{7}{8}$

9. $\frac{5}{9}$ **10.** $\frac{7}{9}$ **11.** $\frac{5}{6}$ **12.** $\frac{4}{5}$

$+ \frac{5}{6}$ $+ \frac{1}{2}$ $+ \frac{3}{4}$ $+ \frac{3}{4}$

13. $\frac{1}{5} + \frac{2}{3} + \frac{5}{6}$ **14.** $\frac{1}{3} + \frac{1}{6} + \frac{8}{9}$ **15.** $\frac{5}{8} + \frac{3}{4} + \frac{3}{10}$

_____   _____   _____

16. Find the sum of $\frac{1}{3}$ and $\frac{7}{8}$. _____

17. Add $\frac{3}{5}$ and $\frac{7}{10}$. _____

18. Find $\frac{1}{3} + \frac{1}{6} + \frac{1}{9} + \frac{1}{12}$ using mental math _____

19. Do you get the same sum when you use 18 rather than 9 as a common denominator for $\frac{2}{3}$ and $\frac{4}{9}$? Explain.

_____

20. What extra step will you have to perform if you do not use the **least common denominator** when adding fractions? Explain your response.

_____

_____

Exploring Subtracting Fractions

1. $\frac{3}{4} - \frac{1}{8} = n$

$\frac{3}{4}$

$\frac{1}{8}$

↓

$\frac{6}{8}$

$\frac{1}{8}$	$\frac{5}{8}$

_____ $- \frac{1}{8} =$ _____

Find each difference. Simplify.

2. $\frac{9}{10} - \frac{3}{5}$

$\frac{9}{10}$

$\frac{3}{5}$

_____

3. $\frac{3}{8} - \frac{1}{4}$

$\frac{3}{8}$

$\frac{1}{4}$

_____

4. $\frac{5}{6} - \frac{3}{4}$

$\frac{5}{6}$

$\frac{3}{4}$

_____

5. $\frac{7}{8} - \frac{1}{6}$

$\frac{7}{8}$

$\frac{1}{6}$

_____

Find each difference. You may use fraction strips or draw pictures to help.

6. $\frac{4}{5} - \frac{1}{10}$

_____

7. $\frac{2}{3} - \frac{2}{9}$

_____

8. $\frac{4}{5} - \frac{8}{15}$

_____

9. $\frac{1}{3} - \frac{1}{6}$

_____

10. $\frac{3}{4} - \frac{1}{6}$

_____

11. $\frac{5}{9} - \frac{1}{3}$

_____

12. $\frac{9}{10} - \frac{3}{5}$

_____

13. $\frac{5}{6} - \frac{1}{4}$

_____

14. $\begin{array}{r} \frac{7}{9} \\ - \frac{2}{3} \\ \hline \end{array}$

15. $\begin{array}{r} \frac{5}{6} \\ - \frac{1}{2} \\ \hline \end{array}$

16. $\begin{array}{r} \frac{5}{7} \\ - \frac{3}{14} \\ \hline \end{array}$

17. $\begin{array}{r} \frac{1}{2} \\ - \frac{1}{8} \\ \hline \end{array}$

18. Find the difference of $\frac{5}{6}$ and $\frac{1}{2}$.
Write the answer in simplest form. _____

Subtracting Fractions

Find each difference. Simplify.

1. $\frac{3}{4} - \frac{1}{3} =$ _____

2. $\frac{2}{3} - \frac{1}{2} =$ _____

3. $\frac{4}{5} - \frac{3}{10} =$ _____

4. $\frac{3}{5} - \frac{1}{10} =$ _____

5. $\frac{7}{8} - \frac{1}{2} =$ _____

6. $\frac{5}{6} - \frac{2}{3} =$ _____

7. $\frac{2}{5} - \frac{1}{5} =$ _____

8. $\frac{5}{6} - \frac{3}{4} =$ _____

9. $\frac{7}{8} - \frac{2}{3} =$ _____

10. $\begin{array}{r} \frac{3}{5} \\ -\ \frac{1}{2} \\ \hline \end{array}$

11. $\begin{array}{r} \frac{7}{12} \\ -\ \frac{1}{6} \\ \hline \end{array}$

12. $\begin{array}{r} \frac{3}{10} \\ -\ \frac{1}{5} \\ \hline \end{array}$

13. $\begin{array}{r} \frac{3}{4} \\ -\ \frac{2}{3} \\ \hline \end{array}$

14. $\begin{array}{r} \frac{7}{8} \\ -\ \frac{1}{4} \\ \hline \end{array}$

15. $\begin{array}{r} \frac{7}{10} \\ -\ \frac{2}{5} \\ \hline \end{array}$

16. $\begin{array}{r} \frac{5}{6} \\ -\ \frac{3}{5} \\ \hline \end{array}$

17. $\begin{array}{r} \frac{5}{7} \\ -\ \frac{1}{3} \\ \hline \end{array}$

18. Find the difference between $\frac{5}{8}$ and $\frac{1}{6}$. _____

19. If $\frac{1}{3}$ is subtracted from $\frac{5}{6}$, will the difference be greater or less than $\frac{1}{3}$? Explain.

_____

_____

20. If $\frac{2}{3}$ is subtracted from $\frac{5}{6}$, will the difference be greater or less than $\frac{1}{3}$? Explain.

_____

_____

Analyze Word Problems:
Too Much or Too Little Information

Write if each problem has too much or too little information.
Solve, or if possible, tell what is needed to solve.

1. During one week, $\frac{1}{3}$ of the hotel rooms were available. The clerk took 20 additional reservations. How many rooms are still available?

_____

_____

2. The school is $\frac{2}{3}$ mi from the library. Jessie lives $\frac{3}{5}$ mi from school. John lives $\frac{1}{10}$ mi closer than Jessie. How far from school is John?

_____

3. Cary cut a hero sandwich into 10 pieces. Only 8 pieces were eaten. His 3 sisters had ravioli. What fraction of the hero sandwich was left?

_____

4. Mom built a shelf. She used $\frac{1}{2}$ a board for the shelf and $\frac{2}{5}$ of the board for the braces. How many inches of the board were left?

_____

_____

5. John rode with his mom in the car $\frac{1}{3}$ mi. He walked the rest of the way to Jim's house. How far did he have to walk?

_____

_____

6. For a recipe Lee needs $\frac{1}{3}$ cup of sugar, $\frac{3}{4}$ cup of flour, and twice as much milk as sugar. How many cups of milk does she need?

_____

Name _____

Review and Practice

Vocabulary Write true or false.

1. The least common denominator (LCD) is the
   least common multiple of the two demoninators. _____

(Lesson 1) Find each sum or difference. Simplify.

2. $\frac{1}{6}$

   $+ \frac{1}{6}$
   _____

3. $\frac{5}{9}$

   $- \frac{2}{9}$
   _____

4. $\frac{10}{11}$

   $- \frac{8}{11}$
   _____

5. $\frac{1}{6}$

   $+ \frac{5}{6}$
   _____

6. What number must be added to $\frac{3}{7}$ to get a sum of 1? _____

(Lessons 2–4) Find each sum. Simplify.

7. $\frac{2}{3} + \frac{1}{9} =$ _____

8. $\frac{1}{4} + \frac{1}{8} =$ _____

9. $\frac{2}{5} + \frac{8}{10} =$ _____

10. $\frac{1}{20} + \frac{1}{5} =$ _____

11. On three days Wendy rode her bike
    $\frac{2}{5}$ mi, $\frac{1}{2}$ mi and $\frac{4}{5}$ mi. How far did she ride? _____

(Lessons 5–6) Find each difference. Simplify.

12. $\frac{8}{9}$

    $- \frac{1}{4}$
    _____

13. $\frac{5}{7}$

    $- \frac{1}{3}$
    _____

14. $\frac{6}{10}$

    $- \frac{1}{3}$
    _____

15. $\frac{5}{8}$

    $- \frac{2}{5}$
    _____

(Lesson 7) Write if the problem has too much or too little information. Solve if possible. Tell what is needed if you can't solve.

16. Sue needed boat line that costs $5 for 6 ft. How much did she spend?

_____

(Mixed Review) Order each list from least to greatest.

17. $\frac{3}{4}, \frac{1}{2}, \frac{4}{6}$ _____

18. $\frac{3}{5}, \frac{2}{7}, \frac{4}{8}$ _____

19. $\frac{5}{7}, \frac{5}{8}, \frac{1}{2}$ _____

Exploring Adding and Subtracting Mixed Numbers

Find each sum or difference. Use fraction strips or drawings to help. Simplify.

1.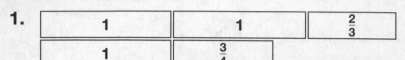

| 1 | 1 | $\frac{2}{3}$ |

| 1 | $\frac{3}{4}$ |

$2\frac{2}{3} + 1\frac{3}{4} =$ _____

2.

| 1 | $\frac{1}{2}$ |

| $\frac{2}{3}$ | ? |

$1\frac{1}{2} - \frac{2}{3} =$ _____

3. $2\frac{2}{3}$
$-\ 1\frac{1}{2}$

4. $3\frac{1}{6}$
$+\ 2\frac{2}{3}$

5. $1\frac{3}{4}$
$+\ \ \frac{1}{12}$

6. $2\frac{3}{10}$
$+\ \ \ \frac{2}{5}$

7. 4
$-\ 2\frac{1}{3}$

8. $3\frac{1}{4}$
$-\ \ \ \frac{2}{16}$

9. $3\frac{1}{6} + 1\frac{2}{3} =$ _____

10. $3\frac{3}{5} - 2\frac{3}{10} =$ _____

11. Find the sum of $2\frac{1}{8}$ and $3\frac{3}{4}$. _____

12. Find the difference of $5\frac{4}{9}$ and $2\frac{1}{3}$. _____

13. How much longer is the pen than the piece of chalk? _____

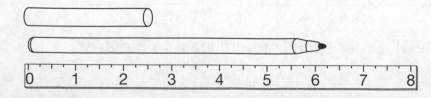

Estimating Sums and Differences

Estimate each sum or difference.

1. $1\frac{1}{3} + 1\frac{1}{6}$

_____

2. $5\frac{1}{8} + 2\frac{1}{2}$

_____

3. $8\frac{1}{2} - 1\frac{1}{4}$

_____

4. $7\frac{4}{5} - 5\frac{1}{4}$

_____

5. $2\frac{3}{4} + 3\frac{2}{3}$

_____

6. $7\frac{3}{4} - 3\frac{1}{2}$

_____

7. $2\frac{1}{2} - 1\frac{1}{8}$

_____

8. $1\frac{1}{3} + 6\frac{1}{12}$

_____

9. $2\frac{3}{5} + 1\frac{2}{3}$

_____

10. $\begin{array}{r} 2\frac{3}{4} \\ + 3\frac{5}{8} \\ \hline \end{array}$

11. $\begin{array}{r} 4\frac{1}{4} \\ - 1\frac{5}{6} \\ \hline \end{array}$

12. $\begin{array}{r} 9\frac{1}{10} \\ - 8\frac{4}{5} \\ \hline \end{array}$

13. $\begin{array}{r} 5\frac{7}{8} \\ + 1\frac{1}{3} \\ \hline \end{array}$

14. $\begin{array}{r} 6\frac{2}{3} \\ - 1\frac{5}{6} \\ \hline \end{array}$

15. $\begin{array}{r} 9\frac{1}{4} \\ - 5 \\ \hline \end{array}$

16. $8\frac{7}{8} + 3\frac{1}{4} + 2\frac{1}{2}$

_____

17. $4\frac{1}{5} + 3\frac{2}{3} + 8\frac{5}{8}$

_____

18. Estimate the difference between $5\frac{1}{8}$ and $2\frac{2}{3}$. _____

Adding and Subtracting Mixed Numbers

Find each sum or difference. Simplify.

1. $4\frac{1}{8}$
$+ \ 3\frac{1}{4}$

2. $4\frac{2}{3}$
$- \ 2\frac{1}{4}$

3. $5\frac{1}{2}$
$- \ 1\frac{1}{5}$

4. $5\frac{1}{3}$
$+ \ 4\frac{1}{8}$

5. $10\frac{3}{10}$
$+ \ \ 9\frac{4}{5}$

6. $14\frac{1}{8}$
$+ \ \ \ \frac{1}{4}$

7. $6\frac{2}{10}$
$- \ 3\frac{1}{5}$

8. $7\frac{1}{3}$
$- \ 5$

9. $3\frac{2}{3}$
$+ \ 4\frac{1}{4}$

10. $6\frac{3}{8}$
$- \ 2\frac{1}{8}$

11. $6\frac{5}{6}$
$- \ 5\frac{1}{3}$

12. $6\frac{5}{6}$
$+ \ 2\frac{1}{3}$

13. $7\frac{2}{3} - 2\frac{1}{6} =$ _____

14. $20\frac{1}{5} + 4\frac{7}{10} =$ _____

15. $8\frac{1}{3} + 8\frac{3}{4} =$ _____

16. $4\frac{5}{8} - 1\frac{1}{2} =$ _____

17. $23\frac{3}{10} + \frac{2}{5} =$ _____

18. $9\frac{3}{8} - 8 =$ _____

19. Find the sum of $6\frac{2}{3}$ and $7\frac{3}{5}$. _____

20. Find the difference of $8\frac{7}{8}$ and $2\frac{3}{4}$. _____

21. How do you simplify $8\frac{9}{6}$?

_____

Adding Mixed Numbers

Find each sum. Simplify, if possible.

1. $2\frac{1}{8}$
$1\frac{1}{2}$
$+\ 3\frac{3}{4}$

2. $5\frac{1}{3}$
$2\frac{1}{2}$
$+\ 1\frac{2}{3}$

3. $3\frac{1}{4}$
$4\frac{1}{2}$
$+\ 1\frac{3}{4}$

4. $6\frac{1}{4}$
$1\frac{1}{2}$
$+\ \ \frac{3}{8}$

5. $9\frac{2}{3}$
$\frac{1}{4}$
$+\ 4\frac{5}{6}$

6. $2\frac{1}{5}$
$4\frac{3}{10}$
$+\ 3\frac{3}{5}$

7. $3\frac{3}{8}$
$2\frac{1}{2}$
$+\ 3\frac{1}{8}$

8. $13\frac{5}{12}$
$8\frac{1}{2}$
$+\ 11$

9. $7 + 4\frac{1}{4} + 6\frac{7}{10} =$ _____

10. $\frac{2}{5} + 4\frac{3}{10} + 1\frac{1}{5} =$ _____

11. $8\frac{1}{8} + 4\frac{7}{10} + \frac{3}{5} =$ _____

12. $3\frac{1}{7} + 21\frac{3}{4} + 3\frac{5}{7} =$ _____

13. $2\frac{1}{2} + 3\frac{1}{4} + 5\frac{1}{8} =$ _____

14. Add $\frac{1}{3}$, $3\frac{3}{5}$, and $7\frac{1}{3}$. _____

15. When adding several fractions you can combine those with common denominators first to make addition easier. How can you combine fractions first to add $2\frac{1}{5}$, $4\frac{1}{4}$, and $3\frac{3}{5}$?

_____

_____

_____

16. Estimation What is $3\frac{5}{7} + 4\frac{1}{8} + 2\frac{3}{4}$ to the nearest whole number?

_____

17. What is the sum of the answers for **1–4**? _____

Subtracting Mixed Numbers

Find each difference. Simplify.

1. $6\frac{1}{3}$
   $-\ 2\frac{3}{4}$

2. $7\frac{3}{4}$
   $-\ 1\frac{3}{8}$

3. $9\frac{1}{2}$
   $-\ \ \ \frac{1}{3}$

4. $6\frac{3}{4}$
   $-\ 4\frac{1}{2}$

5. 7
   $-\ \ \ \frac{3}{5}$

6. $22\frac{1}{3}$
   $-\ 13\frac{3}{8}$

7. 7
   $-\ 2\frac{1}{3}$

8. $6\frac{7}{10}$
   $-\ \ \ \frac{5}{8}$

9. $3\frac{3}{4}$
   $-\ 2\frac{1}{2}$

10. 5
    $-\ 3\frac{3}{4}$

11. $17\frac{4}{9}$
    $-\ 11\frac{5}{6}$

12. $7\frac{1}{8}$
    $-\ 4\frac{4}{5}$

13. $15 - 7\frac{2}{5} =$ _____

14. $11\frac{1}{4} - \frac{5}{8} =$ _____

15. $8\frac{7}{12} - 3\frac{3}{4} =$ _____

16. $5\frac{2}{3} - 2\frac{1}{2} =$ _____

17. $8 - 2\frac{1}{3} =$ _____

18. $17\frac{1}{8} - 4\frac{1}{2} =$ _____

19. Find the difference of $13\frac{2}{5}$ and $3\frac{3}{4}$. _____

20. **Estimation** What is $4\frac{1}{8} - 2\frac{2}{3}$ to the nearest whole number? _____

21. Bridget added $\frac{1}{5}$ to both 12 and $6\frac{4}{5}$ when subtracting $12 - 6\frac{4}{5}$. Tell why.

_____

_____

_____

Compare Strategies: Work Backward/Draw a Picture

Work backward or use any strategy to solve the problem.

1. Stacey, Kiesha, and Maria planned their trip to band camp. Maria had to travel 5 more miles than Kiesha. Stacey had to travel $\frac{1}{2}$ the distance Kiesha traveled. Stacey traveled 50 miles. How far did Maria travel?

   _____

2. Sven and Ryan hiked a desert trail for their scout badge. They followed the trail $1\frac{1}{4}$ miles west, then turned north for $\frac{5}{8}$ mile. Finally they headed east for $1\frac{5}{8}$ mile to join the troop for camp. The next morning they hiked back over the same trail. How many miles in all did they hike? _____

3. Students voted to raise money for new soccer goals for their school. The goals cost $450. Students raised $\frac{1}{3}$ of the money. The school's PTA contributed $50 more than the students. Parents organized an additional fundraiser for the extra funds needed. How much did each group contribute?

   _____

4. Carly, Courtney, and Ashley went to the skating party for their school. Courtney skated three times as many laps as Ashley. Carly skated $\frac{2}{3}$ of the distance Courtney skated. Ashley skated 50 laps. How many laps did Courtney and Carly skate?

   _____

5. Max invited his friends over for pizza. Matt ate 12 slices. Cole ate half as much as Matt but twice as much as Sergio. Max ate 2 more slices than Sergio. How much pizza did Cole, Sergio, and Max each eat?

   _____

Review and Practice

(Lessons 8–12) Find each sum or difference. Simplify.

1. $5\frac{1}{3}$
   $+\ 3\frac{1}{6}$

2. $4\frac{7}{9}$
   $-\ 1\frac{2}{9}$

3. $6\frac{5}{8}$
   $-\ 2\frac{2}{4}$

4. $8\frac{2}{3}$
   $+\ 1\frac{1}{9}$

5. 9
   $-\ \frac{1}{8}$

6. $7\frac{2}{5}$
   $+\ 1\frac{3}{10}$

7. $6\frac{2}{9}$
   $-\ 4\frac{2}{3}$

8. $8\frac{5}{7}$
   $-\ 2\frac{5}{6}$

9. $2\frac{1}{10}$
   $-\ 1\frac{7}{8}$

10. $13\frac{6}{9}$
    $+\ 12\frac{1}{5}$

11. $16\frac{4}{5}$
    $-\ 12\frac{3}{4}$

12. $9\frac{1}{4}$
    $+\ 1\frac{3}{8}$

13. Ms. Whitney bought $2\frac{1}{4}$ yd of red checked material, $1\frac{3}{4}$ yd of blue material, and 3 yd of red material. How many yards of material did she buy in all? _____

(Lesson 13) Solve. Use any strategy.

14. Leroy gave half of his crayons to a friend. He then lost 2. He had 10 left. How many crayons did he have to begin with? _____

15. Trish has a total of 36 colored pencils and chalks. She has 8 more pencils than chalks. How many chalks does she have? _____

(Mixed Review) Tell whether the each is prime or composite.

16. 6 _____
17. 5 _____
18. 27 _____
19. 21 _____
20. 38 _____
21. 31 _____

Linear Measure

Find the length to the nearest $\frac{1}{4}$-inch.

1. _____

2. _____

Find the length to the nearest $\frac{1}{8}$-inch.

3. _____

4. _____

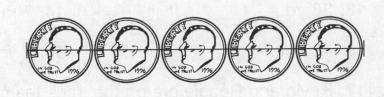

5. Mario broke a pane of glass in a window. The opening measured $7\frac{1}{4}$ in. by $9\frac{1}{2}$ in. At the hardware store, they sold him a pane of glass that was $7\frac{1}{4}$ in. by $9\frac{1}{2}$ in. to the nearest $\frac{1}{4}$ in. Can Mario be sure the glass will fit the window? Explain.

_____

Use your ruler to draw a line segment for each length.

6. $1\frac{3}{4}$ in.

7. $2\frac{1}{8}$ in.

8. $3\frac{1}{4}$ in.

9. $1\frac{1}{8}$ in.

Name _____

Feet, Yards, and Miles

Complete.

1. 12 yd = _____ ft

2. 3 mi = _____ ft

3. 192 in. = _____ ft

4. 2 mi = _____ yd

5. 180 in. = _____ ft

6. 87 in. = _____ ft _____ in.

7. 15 ft 3 in. = _____ in.

8. 21,120 ft = _____ mi

9. 7 ft 4 in. = _____ in.

10. 5 yd 2 ft = _____ ft

11. 63 in. = _____ ft _____ in.

12. 15,840 yd = _____ mi

13. 38 yd = _____ ft

14. 7 mi = _____ ft

15. 420 in. = _____ ft

16. 3 yd 1 ft = _____ ft

17. Kevin and Reggie are on the track team.
Kevin's best high jump is 4 ft 9 in. Reggie's
best jump is 56 in. Who has the better record? _____

18. Complete.

a. Number of feet	21				36	45
b. Number of yards		8	6	4		

c. To change feet to yards, you
must divide the number of feet by _____.

d. To change yards to feet, you must _____ the number
of yards by 3.

19. Complete.

a. Number of inches	12	24	36			
b. Number of feet				5	10	25

c. To change inches to feet you
must divide the number of inches by _____.

d. To change feet to inches you must _____ the number of
feet by 12.

Analyze Word Problems:
Exact or Estimate?

Decide whether you need an exact answer
or an estimate. Solve.

1. Kathy wants to build a bulletin board frame that is $6\frac{1}{8}$ ft wide and 4 ft
high. Would three pieces of wood that are each 8 ft long be enough to
build the frame? Explain your answer.

_____

_____

2. If Kathy wanted to make the frame 2 ft wider and 2 ft higher, would
she have enough wood?

_____

_____

3. Carly usually does gymnastics for three hours on Monday through
Friday, and for two hours on Saturday. About how many hours does
she do gymnastics in a month?

_____

4. Donald needs to be at school band practice by 7:30 A.M. He wants to
get to school at least 15 minutes early. School is about a $\frac{1}{2}$ –hr bike
ride away. What time should Donald leave for school?

_____

5. Sharish saved $210 for a stereo for her room. The stereo costs $186.
Sharish also wanted to purchase two CD's at $11 each. While at the
store, Sharish found another CD she wanted for $13. Did Sharish have
enough money to pay for everything she wanted? Tell what strategy
you used.

_____

_____

Review and Practice

(Lesson 14) Find the length to the nearest $\frac{1}{8}$-inch.

1. _____

2. _____

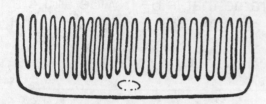

Use your ruler to draw a line segment for each length.

3. $2\frac{3}{4}$ inches

4. $3\frac{7}{8}$ inches

(Lesson 15) Complete.

5. 5 yd = _____ ft

6. 8 ft 7 in. = _____ in.

7. 137 in. = _____ ft _____ in.

8. 3 mi = _____ ft

9. 5 mi = _____ yd

10. 96 in. = _____ ft

11. 6 yd 2 ft = _____ ft

12. 15,840 ft = _____ mi

13. Which is longer, 526 ft or 150 yd? _____

(Lesson 16) Tell whether you need an exact answer or an estimate. Then solve.

14. Betty went to the library at 8:30 A.M. She wants to be at her friend's house by 10:30 A.M. It takes her about 20 minutes to walk to her friend's house. What time should she leave the library?

_____

15. Philip has $12. Does he have enough money to treat himself and two friends to a movie that costs $4? _____

(Mixed Review) Divide.

16. 400 ÷ 2 _____

17. 390 ÷ 3 _____

18. 400 ÷ 20 _____

19. 100 ÷ 50 _____

Cumulative Review

(Chapter 4 Lesson 5) Divide.

1. $6\overline{)726}$

2. $8\overline{)2488}$

3. $5\overline{)834}$

(Chapter 7 Lesson 7) Write in order from least to greatest.

4. $\frac{1}{4}, \frac{5}{6}, \frac{2}{9}$ _____, _____, _____

5. $\frac{2}{3}, \frac{1}{5}, \frac{3}{8}$ _____, _____, _____

6. $\frac{1}{2}, \frac{5}{9}, \frac{2}{5}$ _____, _____, _____

(Chapter 7 Lesson 13) Write each as a percent.

7. 12 out of 100 _____

8. $\frac{31}{100}$ _____

Write each as a hundredths fraction and as a decimal.

9. $\frac{15}{25} =$ _____, _____

10. $\frac{2}{50} =$ _____, _____

(Chapter 8 Lessons 4, 6, and 10) Add or subtract.

11. $\begin{array}{r} \frac{1}{5} \\ + \frac{3}{5} \\ \hline \end{array}$

12. $\begin{array}{r} \frac{7}{8} \\ - \frac{3}{8} \\ \hline \end{array}$

13. $\begin{array}{r} \frac{4}{7} \\ + \frac{2}{7} \\ \hline \end{array}$

14. $\begin{array}{r} \frac{6}{9} \\ - \frac{2}{3} \\ \hline \end{array}$

15. $\begin{array}{r} 3\frac{1}{4} \\ + 2\frac{3}{6} \\ \hline \end{array}$

16. $\begin{array}{r} 4\frac{7}{9} \\ - 1\frac{2}{3} \\ \hline \end{array}$

17. $\begin{array}{r} 5 \\ + \frac{4}{11} \\ \hline \end{array}$

18. $\begin{array}{r} 4 \\ - 1\frac{2}{5} \\ \hline \end{array}$

19. $\begin{array}{r} 3\frac{1}{4} \\ - 1\frac{2}{3} \\ \hline \end{array}$

20. $\begin{array}{r} 8\frac{1}{12} \\ + 3\frac{4}{6} \\ \hline \end{array}$

21. $\begin{array}{r} 4\frac{2}{3} \\ - 1\frac{2}{8} \\ \hline \end{array}$

22. $\begin{array}{r} \frac{6}{7} \\ + 3\frac{1}{6} \\ \hline \end{array}$

Name _____

Exploring Multiplication of Whole Numbers by Fractions

Use division to help you find the fraction of each number.

1. To find $\frac{3}{4}$ of 12, think:

    a. $\frac{1}{4}$ of 12 is ☐.

    b. $\frac{3}{4}$ is 3 times as much as ☐.

    c. $3 \times 3 =$ ☐ so $\frac{3}{4}$ of 12 is ☐.

Find each product. You may use counters to help.

2. $\frac{1}{2}$ of 20 _____   **3.** $\frac{1}{4}$ of 16 _____   **4.** $\frac{3}{4}$ of 24 _____

5. $\frac{1}{9}$ of 27 _____   **6.** $\frac{2}{9}$ of 36 _____   **7.** $\frac{1}{5}$ of 45 _____

8. $\frac{1}{3}$ of 18 _____   **9.** $\frac{4}{5}$ of 15 _____   **10.** $\frac{2}{3}$ of 15 _____

11. Find two-fifths of ten. _____

12. Find four-ninths of 27. _____

13. Find one-third of 21. _____

14. Find two-sevenths of 28. _____

15. Which of the number lines below shows $\frac{1}{5}$ of 50? _____

    a.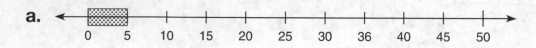

    b.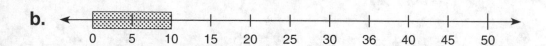

    c.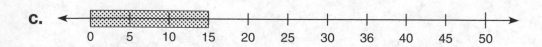

Multiplying with Fractions

Find each product. Use mental math.

1. $\frac{1}{4}$ of 28 _____

2. $\frac{1}{9}$ of 63 _____

3. $\frac{2}{5}$ of 35 _____

4. $\frac{2}{3}$ of 27 _____

5. $\frac{3}{8}$ of 24 _____

6. $\frac{4}{7}$ of 70 _____

7. $\frac{1}{3}$ of 18 _____

8. $\frac{1}{5}$ of 45 _____

9. $\frac{5}{8}$ of 32 _____

10. $\frac{1}{8}$ of 48 _____

11. $\frac{4}{9}$ of 54 _____

12. $\frac{3}{4}$ of 40 _____

13. $\frac{1}{2}$ of 18 _____

14. $\frac{4}{5}$ of 30 _____

15. $\frac{2}{7}$ of 14 _____

16. $\frac{3}{8}$ of 32 _____

17. $\frac{2}{7}$ of 21 _____

18. $\frac{4}{5}$ of 45 _____

19. Multiply one-sixth and sixty. _____

20. Multiply three-fifths and thirty. _____

21. Multiply three-fourths and forty. _____

22. Multiply two-ninths and forty-five. _____

23. Complete the table. Use patterns to help you find each product.

$\frac{1}{6}$ of 36	6	$\frac{4}{6}$ of 36	
$\frac{2}{6}$ of 36	12	$\frac{5}{6}$ of 36	
$\frac{3}{6}$ of 36		$\frac{6}{6}$ of 36	

24. How could you use the product of $\frac{1}{3}$ and 300 to find the product of $\frac{1}{6}$ and 300?

_____

_____

25. How could you use the product of $\frac{1}{2}$ and 200 to find the product of $\frac{1}{8}$ and 200?

_____

_____

Estimating Products

Use rounding, benchmarks, or compatible numbers to estimate each products.

1. $7 \times 2\frac{8}{9}$ _____

2. $\frac{1}{8} \times 17$ _____

3. $\frac{5}{8} \times 10$ _____

4. $\frac{3}{8} \times 22$ _____

5. $1\frac{4}{5} \times 6$ _____

6. $\frac{2}{9} \times 28$ _____

7. $\frac{2}{7} \times 48$ _____

8. $\frac{4}{9} \times 30$ _____

9. $\frac{4}{7} \times 15$ _____

10. $1\frac{7}{8} \times 10$ _____

11. $\frac{4}{5} \times 11$ _____

12. $3\frac{3}{4} \times 4$ _____

13. $\frac{5}{6} \times 25$ _____

14. $\frac{3}{8} \times 33$ _____

15. $2\frac{1}{9} \times 34$ _____

16. Estimate the product of $1\frac{9}{10}$ and 15. Describe your method.

_____

17. Estimate the product of $\frac{2}{3}$ and 31. Describe your method.

_____

18. Estimate the product of $3\frac{7}{8}$ and 25. Describe your method.

_____

Use rounding, benchmarks, or compatible numbers to estimate each product. Write the letter of the estimate that is closer to the actual product.

19. $6 \times 3\frac{7}{8}$ _____   **a.** more than 24   **b.** less than 24

20. $\frac{3}{8} \times 25$ _____   **a.** more than 9   **b.** less than 9

21. $\frac{5}{9} \times 17$ _____   **a.** more than 10   **b.** less than 10

22. $2\frac{1}{7} \times 22$ _____   **a.** more than 44   **b.** less than 44

23. $3\frac{2}{3} \times 10$ _____   **a.** more than 40   **b.** less than 40

Exploring Multiplication of Fractions by Fractions

Use the drawing to help you complete each sentence.

1. $\frac{1}{3} \times \frac{1}{4}$ means $\frac{1}{3}$ of $\frac{1}{4}$

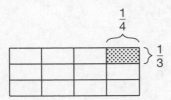

2. $\frac{1}{2} \times \frac{1}{8}$ means $\frac{1}{2}$ of $\frac{1}{8}$

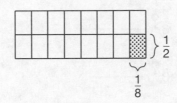

The parts of the rectangle show

that $\frac{1}{4} \times \frac{1}{3} =$ _____

The parts of the rectangle show

that _____ × _____ = _____

3. Which of the drawings below shows $\frac{1}{5} \times \frac{1}{3}$? _____

a.

b.

c.

d.

Use each drawing to help you complete each sentence.

4. $\frac{1}{4}$ is shaded.

$\frac{1}{2}$ of $\frac{1}{4}$ is _____.

5. $\frac{2}{5}$ is shaded.

$\frac{1}{3}$ of $\frac{2}{5}$ is _____.

Draw pictures or use paper folding to find each product.

6. What is $\frac{1}{3} \times \frac{1}{5}$? _____

7. What is $\frac{2}{3}$ of $\frac{1}{5}$? _____

8. $\frac{1}{4} \times \frac{1}{4} =$ _____

9. $\frac{1}{6} \times \frac{1}{2} =$ _____

10. $\frac{3}{4} \times \frac{1}{3} =$ _____

11. $\frac{1}{2} \times \frac{1}{8} =$ _____

12. $\frac{1}{3} \times \frac{1}{7} =$ _____

13. $\frac{2}{3} \times \frac{1}{7} =$ _____

Multiplying Fractions

Find each product. Simplify.

1. What is $\frac{3}{4} \times \frac{1}{3}$? _____

2. What is $\frac{7}{10} \times \frac{1}{2}$? _____

3. What is $\frac{1}{5} \times \frac{2}{3}$? _____

4. What is $\frac{2}{3} \times \frac{1}{5}$? _____

5. What is $\frac{1}{9} \times \frac{2}{3}$? _____

6. What is $\frac{2}{5} \times \frac{3}{6}$? _____

7. $\frac{1}{7} \times \frac{7}{8} =$ _____

8. $\frac{3}{8} \times \frac{1}{4} =$ _____

9. $\frac{2}{3} \times \frac{3}{5} =$ _____

10. $\frac{3}{4} \times \frac{4}{5} =$ _____

11. $\frac{1}{9} \times \frac{9}{10} =$ _____

12. $\frac{3}{7} \times \frac{1}{3} =$ _____

13. $\frac{1}{2} \times \frac{3}{5} =$ _____

14. $\frac{1}{3} \times \frac{3}{8} =$ _____

15. $\frac{5}{6} \times \frac{1}{4} =$ _____

16. $\frac{2}{5} \times \frac{1}{2} =$ _____

17. $\frac{1}{6} \times \frac{6}{7} =$ _____

18. $\frac{2}{9} \times \frac{1}{2} =$ _____

19. $\frac{4}{9} \times \frac{9}{12} =$ _____

20. $\frac{1}{7} \times \frac{5}{7} =$ _____

21. $\frac{11}{12} \times \frac{6}{11} =$ _____

22. $\frac{1}{2}$ is multiplied by a fraction and the product is $\frac{3}{8}$. What is the fraction? _____

23. $\frac{4}{5}$ is multiplied by a fraction and the product is $\frac{4}{15}$. What is the fraction? _____

24. What is the product of $\frac{2}{3}$ and $\frac{3}{3}$? _____

25. Multiply $\frac{1}{2}$ and $\frac{2}{2}$. _____

26. Multiply $\frac{3}{4}$ and $\frac{4}{4}$. _____

27. Multiply $\frac{2}{5}$ and $\frac{5}{5}$. _____

28. Multiply $\frac{8}{8}$ and $\frac{7}{8}$. _____

29. If $\frac{3}{4}$ is multiplied by itself, will the product be greater than $\frac{3}{4}$? Explain.

_____

_____

Analyze Word Problems:
Overestimating and Underestimating

Use overestimating and underestimating to solve the problem.

1. Paula's class washed 22 cars on Saturday afternoon.
   Each customer paid $4.25 for a car wash. Did the class
   earn the $75 they need for a field trip?

   a. Can the problem be solved with an
      estimate or does it require an exact answer? _____

   b. Should you overestimate or underestimate? Why?

      _____

      _____

   c. Did the class earn enough?

      _____

      _____

   d. If the field trip costs $80 instead of $75, how can
      the class be sure that they earned enough? How
      do you know?

      _____

      _____

Estimate to solve. Tell whether you overestimated or
underestimated. Explain your reasoning.

2. Marlene invited 34 people to a party. She will serve
   salad, corn, and $\frac{1}{4}$-pound burgers. How many pounds of
   meat should she buy?

   _____

   _____

Review and Practice

Vocabulary Fill-in each blank with a word from the word bank.

  factor   unit fraction   whole number   numerator   denominator

1. The _____ is the top number of a fraction.

2. A _____ has a 1 as the numerator.

3. One _____ of 8 is 4. Others are 1, 2, and 8.

(Lessons 1 and 2) Find each product.

4. $\frac{1}{3}$ of 24 _____

5. $\frac{1}{9}$ of 36 _____

6. $\frac{10}{11} \times 22 =$ _____

7. $\frac{5}{6} \times 18 =$ _____

8. Find two-thirds of thirty. _____

(Lesson 3) Estimate each product. Use rounding, benchmarks, or compatible numbers.

9. $\frac{3}{4} \times 18$ _____

10. $3\frac{2}{5} \times 32$ _____

11. $2\frac{7}{20} \times 41$ _____

12. $\frac{6}{11} \times 12$ _____

13. $\frac{1}{8}$ of a small box of detergent cleans 1 load of laundry. How many loads could you wash with 5 boxes of detergent?

_____

(Lessons 4 and 5) Find each product.

14. $\frac{8}{9} \times \frac{1}{4} =$ _____

15. $\frac{5}{7} \times \frac{3}{4} =$ _____

16. $\frac{6}{10} \times \frac{5}{12} =$ _____

17. $\frac{3}{8} \times \frac{8}{9} =$ _____

Complete.

18. $\frac{1}{3}$ of _____ $= \frac{1}{9}$

19. $\frac{1}{6}$ of _____ $= \frac{5}{42}$

(Mixed Review) Round each to the nearest whole number.

20. $2\frac{1}{3}$ _____

21. $6\frac{3}{8}$ _____

22. 5.75 _____

23. 6.09 _____

24. $14\frac{7}{8}$ _____

25. 2.49 _____

Multiplying Whole Numbers by Fractions

Complete.

1. $\frac{5}{8} \times 3 = \frac{\boxed{}}{8} = 1\frac{7}{8}$

2. $\frac{2}{7} \times 5 = \frac{\boxed{}}{7} = 1\frac{3}{7}$

3. $\frac{3}{5} \times 9 = \frac{\boxed{}}{5} = \boxed{}$

4. $\frac{3}{4} \times 7 = \frac{\boxed{}}{4} = \boxed{}$

5. $\frac{3}{4} \times 8 = \frac{\boxed{}}{\boxed{}} = \boxed{}$

6. $5 \times \frac{8}{10} = \frac{\boxed{}}{\boxed{}} = \boxed{}$

7. $9 \times \frac{5}{9} = \frac{\boxed{}}{\boxed{}} = \boxed{}$

8. $4 \times \frac{9}{12} = \frac{\boxed{}}{\boxed{}} = \boxed{}$

Find each product.

9. $\frac{7}{6} \times 6 =$ _____

10. $\frac{2}{3} \times 9 =$ _____

11. $\frac{8}{9} \times 7 =$ _____

12. $\frac{3}{7} \times 49 =$ _____

13. $\frac{1}{3} \times 96 =$ _____

14. $\frac{9}{8} \times 11 =$ _____

15. $\frac{4}{5} \times 30 =$ _____

16. $\frac{2}{9} \times 54 =$ _____

17. $\frac{4}{3} \times 24 =$ _____

18. $\frac{8}{7} \times 63 =$ _____

19. $\frac{6}{7} \times 28 =$ _____

20. $\frac{3}{5} \times 60 =$ _____

21. Explain how you can find the product of 5 and $\frac{3}{4}$.

_____

22. Complete. $4 \times \frac{3}{4} = 3$, so $\frac{3}{4} \times 4 = \boxed{}$.

23. James says that he knows all the answers to the following problems are mixed numbers, even without solving them. Explain how he knows.

$\frac{3}{5} \times 248$ $\frac{5}{9} \times 366$ $\frac{7}{8} \times 450$

_____

_____

Multiplying Whole Numbers and Mixed Numbers

Complete.

1. $8\frac{2}{3} \times 7 = \frac{\boxed{}}{3} \times 7$

2. $4\frac{1}{8} \times 6 = \frac{\boxed{}}{8} \times 6$

3. $4 \times 5\frac{1}{3} = 4 \times \frac{\boxed{}}{3}$

4. $9 \times 6\frac{7}{8} = 9 \times \frac{\boxed{}}{8}$

5. $7\frac{7}{8} \times 3\frac{3}{4} = \frac{\boxed{}}{8} \times \frac{\boxed{}}{4}$

6. $3\frac{4}{7} \times 2\frac{7}{9} = \frac{\boxed{}}{7} \times \frac{\boxed{}}{9}$

Find each product. Simplify. Use estimation to check.

7. $7\frac{8}{9} \times 3 =$ _____

8. $8 \times 2\frac{2}{3} =$ _____

9. $2\frac{3}{4} \times 12 =$ _____

10. $2\frac{7}{9} \times 4 =$ _____

11. $2\frac{7}{8} \times 8 =$ _____

12. $4 \times 3\frac{1}{6} =$ _____

13. $10 \times 4\frac{1}{8} =$ _____

14. $3\frac{5}{6} \times 7 =$ _____

15. $\frac{2}{3} \times 1\frac{7}{10} =$ _____

16. $2\frac{1}{4} \times \frac{8}{9} =$ _____

17. $3\frac{1}{2} \times \frac{7}{8} =$ _____

18. $5\frac{2}{3} \times \frac{2}{5} =$ _____

19. $3\frac{1}{2} \times 2\frac{2}{5} =$ _____

20. $3\frac{3}{8} \times 4\frac{1}{3} =$ _____

21. $\frac{2}{9} \times 4\frac{3}{8} =$ _____

22. $4\frac{5}{7} \times 2\frac{8}{9} =$ _____

23. Find the product of $2\frac{1}{3}$ and $3\frac{1}{8}$. _____

24. Find the product of $4\frac{2}{3}$ and $7\frac{5}{6}$. _____

25. Find the product of $1\frac{3}{7}$ and 9. _____

26. Multiply $2\frac{2}{3}$ and $7\frac{3}{8}$. _____

27. Multiply $3\frac{9}{10}$ and $2\frac{2}{5}$. _____

28. Multiply $8\frac{6}{7}$ and $3\frac{2}{7}$. _____

Compare Strategies:
Logical Reasoning/Draw a Picture

Use logical reasoning to solve the problem.

1. Rosa, Gina, Bryan, and Patrick are each wearing their favorite
color shirt: blue, pink, green, or red. No one likes a color that begins
with the same letter as his or her name. Neither Gina nor
Bryan likes red. Gina's pink shoes match her shirt. Which person is
wearing each color?

	Rosa	Gina	Bryan	Patrick
Red				
Green				
Blue				
Pink				

Use logical reasoning or any strategy to solve each problem.

2. Luis said, "Guess my birthday. I was born in a summer month
whose name does not begin with J. The day is a 2-digit number
that is a multiple of 7. My birthday is close to the middle of
the month." When is Luis's birthday?

_____

3. Amy's ancestors came to America in the 1800s. Amy asked
her mom what the exact year was. Her mom said, "The digit in
the tens place is half the digit in the hundreds place. The digit
in the ones place is 3 more than the digit in the tens place."
What year did they come to America?

_____

4. LaVonne goes to bed at 9:00. She has 2 hours of homework.
Dinner will take 30 minutes, and washing the dishes will take 15
minutes. She wants to watch $1\frac{1}{2}$ hours of TV and work on the
computer for 45 minutes.

a. What time should she start doing all these things? _____

b. What strategy did you use to solve this problem?

_____

Exploring Division of Fractions

Complete the drawings to find each quotient.

1. How many $\frac{1}{2}$'s are in 3? _____

2. How many $\frac{1}{3}$'s are in 2? _____

3. How many $\frac{1}{4}$'s are in 4? _____

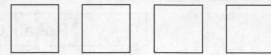

4. How many $\frac{1}{6}$'s are in 5? _____

Find each quotient.

5. How many $\frac{1}{2}$'s are in 9? _____

6. How many $\frac{1}{6}$'s are in 5? _____

7. How many $\frac{1}{4}$'s are in 14? _____

8. $10 \div \frac{1}{8} =$ _____   **9.** $11 \div \frac{1}{4} =$ _____

10. $4 \div \frac{1}{11} =$ _____   **11.** $6 \div \frac{1}{3} =$ _____

12. $8 \div \frac{1}{10} =$ _____   **13.** $15 \div \frac{1}{4} =$ _____

14. $9 \div \frac{1}{6} =$ _____   **15.** $12 \div \frac{1}{5} =$ _____

16. $7 \div \frac{1}{4} =$ _____   **17.** $7 \div \frac{1}{7} =$ _____

18. Cheesy Pizza cuts all large pizzas into twelfths. How many pieces of pizza would Alicia get if she orders 3 large pizzas?

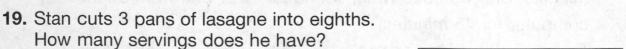

19. Stan cuts 3 pans of lasagne into eighths. How many servings does he have? _____

20. For a fruit plate, Jay cuts 6 apples into sixths. How many pieces of apple does he have? _____

Name _____

Review and Practice

(Lessons 7 and 8) Find each product. Simplify.

1. $\frac{2}{3} \times 9 =$ _____

2. $\frac{7}{9} \times \frac{9}{10} =$ _____

3. $\frac{5}{8} \times \frac{4}{5} =$ _____

4. $\frac{2}{7} \times \frac{1}{4} =$ _____

5. $2\frac{1}{2} \times 6 =$ _____

6. $\frac{1}{7} \times 6\frac{2}{9} =$ _____

7. $2\frac{2}{5} \times \frac{4}{6} =$ _____

8. $2\frac{2}{7} \times 1\frac{3}{4} =$ _____

9. Kim can walk $\frac{2}{3}$ of a mile in 15 minutes.
How far can she walk in $\frac{1}{3}$ of the time? _____

(Lesson 9) Solve each problem.

10. Phil, Mel, Shel, and Cal are a pharmacist, machinist, secretary, and chef. No one has an occupation that begins with the same letter as his or her name. Neither Phil nor Mel is a chef. Cal is a secretary. What is the occupation of each person?

_____

_____

11. What fraction of an hour is 40 minutes? _____

(Lesson 10) Find each quotient.

12. $4 \div \frac{1}{3} =$ _____

13. $5 \div \frac{1}{4} =$ _____

14. $20 \div \frac{1}{10} =$ _____

15. $17 \div \frac{1}{2} =$ _____

16. $18 \div \frac{1}{5} =$ _____

17. $13 \div \frac{1}{7} =$ _____

18. How many $\frac{1}{4}$'s are in 9? _____

19. How many $\frac{1}{3}$'s are in 12? _____

(Mixed Review) Find each sum.

20. $\frac{6}{9} + \frac{1}{9} =$ _____

21. $\frac{2}{5} + \frac{3}{5} =$ _____

22. $\frac{1}{8} + \frac{5}{8} =$ _____

23. $\frac{2}{7} + \frac{3}{7} =$ _____

Cumulative Review

(Chapter 5 Lesson 10) Divide. Round each answer to the nearest cent if needed.

1. $16\overline{)\$7.26}$ **2.** $28\overline{)\$244.88}$ **3.** $35\overline{)\$68.34}$

(Chapter 7 Lesson 3) Write each as an equivalent fraction with a denominator of 12.

4. $\frac{2}{3}$ _____ **5.** $\frac{12}{24}$ _____

6. $\frac{5}{6}$ _____ **7.** $\frac{3}{4}$ _____

(Chapter 8 Lesson 12) Find each difference.

8. $3\frac{1}{4}$
$-\ 2\frac{3}{6}$

9. $3\frac{5}{9}$
$-\ 1\frac{2}{3}$

10. $5\frac{6}{7}$
$-\ \ \ \frac{4}{5}$

11. $3\frac{3}{4}$
$-\ 1\frac{1}{3}$

12. $6\frac{1}{3}$
$-\ 3\frac{4}{6}$

13. $4\frac{2}{5}$
$-\ 1\frac{2}{8}$

(Chapter 8 Lesson 15) Complete.

14. 12 yd = _____ ft **15.** 2 mi = _____ ft

16. 13 ft 7 in. = _____ in. **17.** 3 yd 2 ft = _____ ft

18. 34 in. = _____ ft _____ in.

(Chapter 9 Lessons 7 and 8) Find each product.

19. $\frac{4}{5} \times 15 =$ _____ **20.** $\frac{3}{7} \times \frac{7}{8} =$ _____

21. $\frac{7}{9} \times \frac{3}{14} =$ _____ **22.** $\frac{1}{6} \times \frac{3}{4} =$ _____

23. $3\frac{1}{2} \times 16 =$ _____ **24.** $2\frac{4}{5} \times 2\frac{1}{7} =$ _____

25. $3\frac{1}{3} \times 3\frac{3}{8} =$ _____ **26.** $4\frac{1}{6} \times \frac{2}{3} =$ _____

Exploring Estimating and Measuring Length

Draw a line to match each distance estimate to the most appropriate unit of measurement listed.

1. The distance covered by driving from St. Louis, Missouri to Louisville, Kentucky

2. The distance between 2 leaves on the same branch of a tree

3. The distance you cover when crossing a parking lot

4. The distance between two rows of desks in a classroom

a. centimeters

b. decimeters

c. meters

d. kilometers

Choose the most appropriate unit of measure to estimate the length or height of each. Write cm, dm, or m.

5. _____

6. _____

7. _____

8. _____

Choose the most appropriate unit of measure to estimate the length or height of each. Write m or km.

9.

_____

10.

_____

11.

_____

12.

_____

Millimeters

Complete.

1. 90 mm = _____ cm   **2.** 3 dm = _____ mm

3. 1,400 mm = _____ cm   **4.** 6 m = _____ dm

5. 50 cm = _____ mm   **6.** 200 cm = _____ dm

7. 9 m = _____ dm   **8.** 8,000 mm = _____ m

9. 40 mm = _____ cm   **10.** 3,000 mm = _____ dm

11. 200 cm = _____ dm   **12.** 4,000 mm = _____ cm

13. 900 cm = _____ mm   **14.** 50 dm = _____ mm

15. 6 m = _____ cm   **16.** 7,000 mm = _____ m

17. 20 m = _____ cm   **18.** 8 cm = _____ mm

19. 17 cm = _____ mm   **20.** 5 m = _____ mm

21. 100 cm = _____ m   **22.** 6 dm = _____ cm

23. The width of a hockey puck is 44 mm. Is this length
shorter or longer than 5 cm? Explain.

_____

24. Old Faithful, Yellowstone National Park's most famous
geyser, shoots a spray of steam and hot water 50 m into
the air. Is this height greater or less than 5,000 mm?
Explain.

_____

Centimeters, Meters, and Decimals

Complete.

1. 0.42 m = _____ cm   **2.** 76 cm = _____ m

3. 388 cm = _____ m   **4.** 56 m = _____ cm

5. 6.76 m = _____ cm   **6.** 552 cm = _____ m

Write each measurement, first in centimeters only and then in meters only.

7. 6 m 80 cm _____

8. 5 m 29 cm _____

9. 6 m 17 cm _____

10. 8 m 67 cm _____

Write the longer distance.

11. The length of a football field (91 m) or the distance from the pitcher's mound to home plate (1,844 cm)

_____

12. The length of a kangaroo's hop (7.6 m) or the length of a frog's jump (1,000 cm)

_____

13. The length of the longest dinosaur (3,000 cm) or the length of the ocean liner Queen Elizabeth II (293.5 m)

_____

14. The height of the Eiffel Tower in Paris (300.5 m) or the height of the Empire State Building in New York City (38,100 cm)

_____

Millimeters, Centimeters, and Decimals

Complete.

1. 4.7 cm = _____ mm

2. 46 cm = _____ mm

3. 42 cm = _____ mm

4. 80 mm = _____ cm

5. 3 mm = _____ cm

6. 49 m = _____ cm

7. 9.78 cm = _____ mm

8. 32.1 cm = _____ mm

9. 4,321 cm = _____ m

10. 82.4 mm = _____ cm

11. 9.10 m = _____ cm

12. 849.2 cm = _____ mm

13. Which length is the longest?

_____

A. 94 mm

B. 9.4 cm

C. 9.40 m

14. Which length is the longest?

_____

A. 6.7 m

B. 67 cm

C. 670 m

15. Which length is the shortest?

_____

A. 0.19 m

B. 1.9 cm

C. 190 mm

16. Which length is the shortest?

_____

A. 6,205 mm

B. 6.205 m

C. 62.05 cm

17. Which two lengths are equal?

_____

A. 2.3 m

B. 230 cm

C. 230 mm

18. Which two lengths are equal?

_____

A. 4,867 mm

B. 486.7 cm

C. 48.67 m

Name _____

Review and Practice

Vocabulary Fill in each blank with the correct word.

meter   decimeter   centimeter

1. One tenth of a meter is equal to 1 _____.

2. 1,000 millimeters is equal to one _____.

3. One meter is equal to 100 _____.

(Lesson 1) Circle the most appropriate unit of measure to estimate each.

4. length of a golf club   mm   m   km

5. thickness of a dime   mm   cm   dm

6. distance to a museum   dm   m   km

(Lesson 2) Complete.

7. 8 m = _____ cm   **8.** 500 cm = _____ m

9. 90 dm = _____ m   **10.** 3,000 mm = _____ m

(Lesson 3) Write each measurement, first in centimeters only and then in meters only.

11. 9 m 15 cm _____

12. 4 m 30 cm _____

13. 12 m 8 cm _____

(Lesson 4) Complete.

14. 2.5 mm = _____ cm   **15.** 6.3 cm = _____ mm

16. 16.03 m = _____ cm   **17.** 9.8 m = _____ cm

(Mixed Review) Find each product.

18. $3 \times \frac{3}{5}$ = _____   **19.** $\frac{2}{3} \times \frac{6}{7}$ = _____

20. 3.58 × 10 = _____   **21.** 46.17 × 100 = _____

22.   2.7 5
      × 0.0 0 0 4

23.   3.2 2
      × 0.0 0 5

24.   5.8 6
      × 0.0 0 0 0 3

Exploring Perimeter of Polygons

Write a multiplication number sentence describing the
perimeter of each polygon.

1. 7 cm ⟋△⟍ 7 cm
7 cm

_____

2. 8 yd
8 yd ☐ 8 yd
8 yd

_____

3. 3 m
3 m ⟨⬡⟩ 3 m
3 m   3 m
3 m

_____

Find each perimeter.

4. 5 dm ⟋◺⟍ 7 dm
9 dm

_____

5. ⬠
2 ft

_____

6. ⬓ 20 mm
40 mm

_____

7. 2 m
5 m
7 m   2 m
2 m
4 m

_____

8.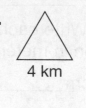
4 m 5 m 3 m
6 m   1 m
3 m
2 m 2 m

_____

9. △
4 km

_____

10. a regular pentagon with sides of 9 cm _____

11. a triangle with sides of 8 dm, 8 dm and 10 dm _____

12. a regular hexagon with sides of 5 mm _____

13. an equilateral triangle with sides of 4 cm _____

14. When finding the perimeter of a regular polygon, will you get the same
answer if you add each side as when you multiply the length of one
side by the total number of sides? Explain.

_____

_____

Name _____

Exploring Perimeter of Rectangles

Use the formula $P = 2 \times (l + w)$ to find the perimeter of each rectangle. Fill in the missing numbers.

1.
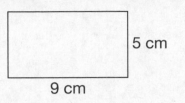
5 cm

9 cm

$P = 2 \times ($ _____ $+$ _____ $)$

$P = 2 \times ($ _____ $)$

$P =$ _____ cm

2.
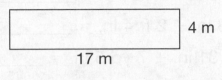
4 m

17 m

$P = 2 \times ($ _____ $+$ _____ $)$

$P = 2 \times ($ _____ $)$

$P =$ _____ m

Find the perimeter of each rectangle.

3.
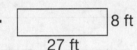
8 ft

27 ft

_____

4.
16 cm

31 cm

_____

5.
2.3 m

3.4 m

_____

6. $l = 26$ ft

$w = 24$ ft

$P =$ _____

7. $l = 246$ mi

$w = 93$ mi

$P =$ _____

8. $l = 4.25$ m

$w = 3.85$ m

$P =$ _____

Estimate the perimeter of each rectangle.

9.
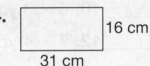
47.6 m

118.5 m

_____

10.
476 yd

526 yd

_____

11.
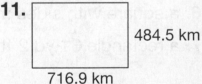
484.5 km

716.9 km

_____

12. What is the perimeter of a rectangular rose garden 5.3 meters long and 3.7 meters wide? _____

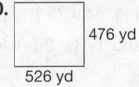

Converting Units to Find Perimeter

Find each sum.

1. 3 yd 2 ft + 2 yd 1 ft = _____

2. 8 ft 8 in. + 2 ft 4 in. = _____

3. 6 yd 31 in. + 7 yd 5 in. = _____

4. 3 yd 2 ft + 5 yd 2 ft = _____

5. 9 ft 3 in. + 8 ft 11 in. = _____

6. 11 yd 1 ft + 3 yd 2 ft = _____

Find each product.

7. 3 × 4 ft 6 in. = _____   **8.** 2 × 6 ft 5 in. = _____

9. 5 × 2 yd 9 in. = _____   **10.** 6 × 3 yd 2 ft = _____

11. 4 × 11 yd 2 ft = _____   **12.** 7 × 4 yd 9 in. = _____

13. Find the perimeter of a
bird house 2 ft 7 in. by 1 ft 5 in. _____

14. Find the perimeter of a square
sandbox with sides measuring 7 ft 8 in. _____

Find each perimeter.

15. a rectangle 6 ft 10 in. long and 4 ft 11 in. wide _____

16. a square with sides measuring 2 mi 25 ft _____

17. a rectangle 31 yd 2 ft long and 17 yd 2 ft wide _____

18. Which rectangle has the greater perimeter? Explain how you know.

a.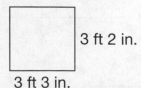
3 ft 2 in.

3 ft 3 in.

b.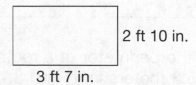
2 ft 10 in.

3 ft 7 in.

Exploring Area of Rectangles

Use the formula $A = l \times w$ to find the area of each rectangle. Fill in the missing numbers.

1.

7 ft

9 ft

$A = $ _____ $\times$ _____

$A = $ _____ ft^2

2.

6 yd

8 yd

$A = $ _____ $\times$ _____

$A = $ _____ yd^2

Find the area of each square.

Use the formula $A = s^2$ to find the area of each square. Fill in the missing numbers.

3.

11 in.

11 in.

a. $A = $ _____ ^{2}

b. $A = $ _____

4.

17 cm

17 cm

a. $A = $ _____ ^{2}

b. $A = $ _____

Find the area of each rectangle.

5. $l = 14$ mi
$w = 8$ mi

$A = $ _____

6. $l = 3.9$ m
$w = 5$ m

$A = $ _____

7. $l = 16$ m
$w = 0.5$ m

$A = $ _____

8. $s = 13$ cm

$A = $ _____

9. $l = 18$ ft

$w = 12$ ft

$A = $ _____

10. $s = 15$ yd

$A = $ _____

11. A rectangle has an area of 91 m^2 and a length of 13 m. What is its width? _____

12. A square has an area of 144 cm^2. What is the measure of its side? _____

Decision Making

You would like to participate in an after-school activity.
The following is a list of things you might do.

Activity	Cost	Time
Sports Team	$50 for uniform	3:45 P.M. – 5 P.M., Mon., Wed., Fri., Sat.
Dance Class	$12.75 a class	3:45 P.M. – 5 P.M., Tue., Thur.
Music Lesson	$30 a week	3 P.M. – 4 P.M., Mon., Wed.
Arts and Crafts	$40 a month	12 P.M. – 5 P.M., Sat.

1. Which activity is the most expensive for a month?
   the least?

   _____

2. If you wanted to participate in as many activities as you
   could, which activities could you choose? Explain.

   _____

   _____

3. How much would it cost in a month to participate in
   these activities? Find the cost for each.

   _____

   _____

4. a. Which activities would you choose?

   _____

   _____

   b. How much would it cost for one month?

   _____

Review and Practice

Vocabulary Write a definition for each word.

1. perimeter _____

_____

2. area _____

_____

(Lessons 5–7) Find each perimeter.

3.   3 in.   7 in.   5 in.

_____

4.   2 cm   9 cm

_____

5.   5 mm   3 mm   3 mm   5 mm
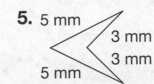

_____

6. $\frac{1}{3}$ in. $\frac{1}{3}$ in.

_____

7.   3 ft 2 in.   14 ft 3 in.

_____

8.   20 mm   40 mm

_____

(Lesson 8) Find each area.

9.   5 ft   5 ft

_____

10.   50 cm   80 cm

_____

11. $\frac{3}{4}$ in. $\frac{5}{6}$ in.

_____

(Mixed Review) Complete.

12. $300 \times$ _____ $= 1,800$

13. $36,000 \div$ _____ $= 4,000$

14. $16 \times$ _____ $= 320$

15. $45,000 \div$ _____ $= 50$

Exploring Area of Right Triangles

Use the formula $A = \frac{1}{2} \times (b \times h)$ to find the area of each right triangle. Fill in the missing numbers.

1.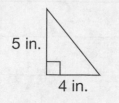

5 in.

4 in.

$A = \frac{1}{2} \times ($ _____ $\times$ _____ $)$

$A = \frac{1}{2} \times ($ _____ $)$

$A = $ _____ in²

2.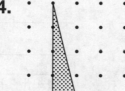

2 m

8 m

$A = \frac{1}{2} \times ($ _____ $\times$ _____ $)$

$A = \frac{1}{2} \times ($ _____ $)$

$A = $ _____ m²

Find each area.

3.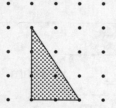

_____

4.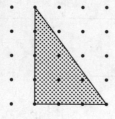

_____

5.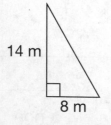

_____

6.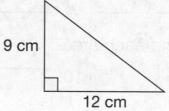

9 cm

12 cm

_____

7.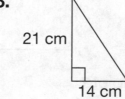

14 m

8 m

_____

8.

21 cm

14 cm

_____

Exploring Area of Triangles

Use the formula $A = \frac{1}{2} \times (b \times h)$ to find the area of each triangle. Fill in the missing numbers.

1.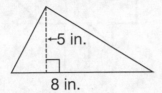

$A = \frac{1}{2} \times ($ _____ $\times$ _____ $)$

$A = \frac{1}{2} \times ($ _____ $)$

$A =$ _____ in^2

2.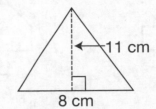

$A = \frac{1}{2} \times ($ _____ $\times$ _____ $)$

$A = \frac{1}{2} \times ($ _____ $)$

$A =$ _____ cm^2

Find each area.

3.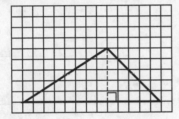

$A =$ _____ units^2

4.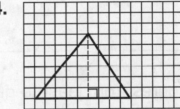

$A =$ _____ units^2

5.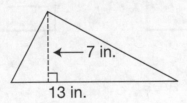

$A =$ _____ in^2

6.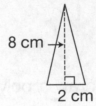

$A =$ _____ cm^2

7. Alyson planted a garden area in the shape of a triangle. The base was 9 ft and the height was 7 ft. What was the area of the triangular garden? _____

8. Rosey embroidered triangles on a pillow cover. Each triangle has a base of 2 in. and a height of 3 in. What is the area of each triangle? _____

Name _____

Exploring Area of Other Polygons

Find each area.

1.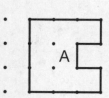

2.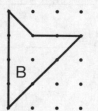

3.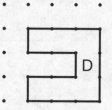

_____ _____ _____

Find each area.

4.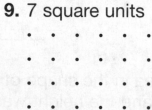

5.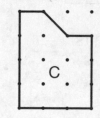

6.

_____ _____ _____

7. Order the figures from least to greatest area. ____, ____, ____, ____

A   B   C   D

On dot paper below, draw a polygon with each area.

8. 6 square units

9. 7 square units

10. $4\frac{1}{2}$ square units

Exploring Area of Parallelograms

Use the formula $A = b \times h$ to find the area of each
parallelogram. Fill in the missing numbers.

1.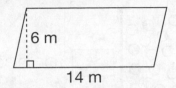

6 m

14 m

$A =$ _____ × _____

$A =$ _____ m²

2.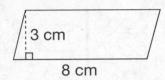

3 cm

8 cm

$A =$ _____ × _____

$A =$ _____ cm²

Find each area.

3.

_____

4.

_____

5.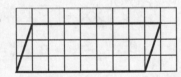

_____

6.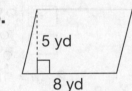

5 yd

8 yd

_____

7.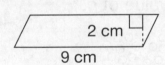

2 cm

9 cm

_____

8.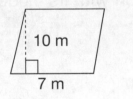

10 m

7 m

_____

Find each missing base or height.

9.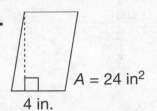

$A = 24$ in²

4 in.

_____

10.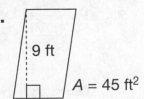

9 ft

$A = 45$ ft²

_____

11.

4.6 cm

$A = 39.1$ cm²

_____

Exploring Algebra: Balancing Equations

Find the number of counters in each envelope. Fill in the missing numbers.

1.

$n + 7 = 12$ $n = 5$

2.

$3 \times n = 18$ $n = 6$

Find the value of n.
Subtract 7 from both sides.

a. $n + 7 - $ _____ $= 12 - $ _____

b. $n = $ _____

c. Check _____ $+ 7 = 12$

Find the value of n.
Divide both sides by 3.

a. $(3 \times n) \div $ _____ $= 18 \div $ _____

b. $n = $ _____

c. Check $3 \times $ _____ $= 18$

Use counters to find the number of counters in each envelope.

3.

$6 + n = 15$

$n = $ _____

4.

$2 \times n = 10$

$n = $ _____

5.

$8 = 4 + n$

$n = $ _____

Match each equation with its model. Then find the value of n.

6. $n + 8 = 21$

$n = $ _____

7. $2 \times n = 20$

$n = $ _____

8. $n + 8 = 15$

$n = $ _____

9. $2 \times n = 32$

$n = $ _____

a.

b.

c.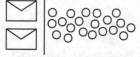

d.

Analyze Strategies: Look for a Pattern

Look for a pattern to solve the problem.

1. The bells at Madison Middle School ring at 8:25, 9:15, 10:05, and 10:55. If this pattern continues, when will the next 4 bells ring?

   a. How much time elapses between the first 2 bells? _____

   b. How much time elapses between the 2nd and 3rd bells? _____

   the 3rd and 4th bells? _____

   c. What is the pattern? _____

   d. Continue the pattern. When will the next 4 bells ring?

   _____

Look for a pattern or use any strategy to help solve each problem.

2. Kimberly is planning to make 1 beaded necklace on Monday, 2 beaded necklaces on Tuesday, 4 on Wednesday, and 8 on Thursday. If this pattern continues, how many necklaces will she make on Sunday? _____

3. Kineesha packed these things for a trip: a white blouse, a pink blouse, a blue blouse, white shorts, a red skirt, and blue jeans. How many different outfits can Kineesha wear? _____

4. To be sure to have enough baked potatoes, Stu is preparing 3 for every pair of guests. If he has invited 48 people, how many potatoes will he bake? _____

5. Aimee's clock was 5 minutes slow on May 1, 7 minutes slow on May 2, 10 minutes slow on May 3, 14 minutes slow on May 4, and 19 minutes slow on May 5. If this pattern continues, what is the first day the clock will be more than an hour slow? _____

Exploring Circumference

Use the formula $C = \pi \times d$ to find the circumference of each circle. Fill in the missing numbers.

1.

2.

$C = 3.14 \times$ _____

$C = 2 \times 3.14 \times$ _____

$C =$ _____ in.

$C =$ _____ cm

Find each circumference. Use 3.14 for π.

3. $C =$ _____

4. $C =$ _____

5. $C =$ _____

Find each diameter to the nearest hundredth. Use 3.14 for π.

6. $C = 16$ ft

7. $C = 22$ in.

8. $C = 48$ mm

$d =$ _____

$d =$ _____

$d =$ _____

Find each radius to the nearest hundredth. Use 3.14 for π.

9. $C = 52$ in.

10. $C = 73$ ft

11. $C = 62$ m

$r =$ _____

$r =$ _____

$r =$ _____

Review and Practice

Vocabulary Draw an example of each on a separate sheet of paper.

1. diameter

2. radius

3. height of a triangle

(Lessons 10–13) Find the area of each figure.

4.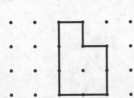

5.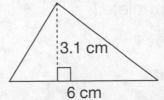
3.1 cm
6 cm

6.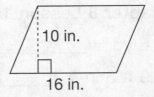
10 in.
16 in.

_____   _____   _____

(Lesson 14) Find the value of *n*. You may use counters to help.

7.

$n + 8 = 11$

$n =$ _____

8.

$5 + n = 13$

$n =$ _____

(Lesson 16) Find each circumference. Use 3.14 for π.

9.

8

$C =$ _____

10.

1.5

$C =$ _____

11.

4.3

$C =$ _____

(Mixed Review) Divide.

12. $7\overline{)945}$

13. $6\overline{)735}$

14. $5\overline{)862}$

Cumulative Review

(Chapter 3 Lesson 13) Find each product. Round to the nearest cent where necessary.

1. 1 6.2	**2.** $3 8.1 5	**3.** $4.0 2	**4.** 3.0 4 1
× 2.4	× 5.7	× 5 3	× 7.8

(Chapter 8 Lesson 15) Complete.

5. 6 yd = _____ ft

6. 9 ft 3 in. = _____ in.

7. 28 in. = _____ ft _____ in.

8. 133 in. _____ ft _____ in.

(Chapter 9 Lesson 5) Find each product.

9. $\frac{3}{4} \times \frac{2}{7} =$ _____

10. $\frac{2}{3} \times \frac{9}{21} =$ _____

11. $\frac{3}{8} \times \frac{8}{7} =$ _____

12. $\frac{6}{10} \times \frac{20}{30} =$ _____

(Chapter 9 Lesson 10) Find each quotient.

13. $6 \div \frac{1}{2} =$ _____

14. $9 \div \frac{1}{4} =$ _____

15. $15 \div \frac{1}{3} =$ _____

16. $8 \div \frac{1}{10} =$ _____

(Chapter 10 Lesson 4) Complete.

17. 38 mm = _____ cm

18. 18 cm = _____ mm

19. 9.3 m = _____ cm

20. 472 cm = _____ m

(Chapter 10 Lesson 8) Find each area.

21. a square with sides that measure 12 feet _____

22. a rectangle with length 1.5 m and width 5 m _____

Exploring Solids

Complete the table comparing a pyramid and a prism.

	Solid	Number of Bases	Shape of Side Faces
1.			
2.	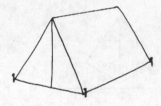		

Write the name of the solid suggested in each drawing.

3.

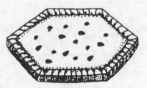

_____

4.

_____

5.

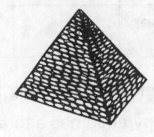

_____

6.

_____

Decide if each statement is true *always*, *sometimes*, or *never*.

7. A pyramid has 2 bases. _____

8. A prism has 2 bases. _____

9. A pyramid has 4 faces. _____

10. A pentagonal pyramid has 5 triangular faces. _____

11. A triangular prism has 3 square faces. _____

12. The side faces of a pyramid are triangles. _____

Exploring Patterns with Solids

Complete the rule you discovered for prisms. Then solve the problems.

1. For any prism, number of _____ + number

   of vertices = number of edges + _____.

2. A pentagonal prism has 7 faces and 10 vertices. How many edges does it have? _____

3. An octagonal prism has 16 vertices and 24 edges. How many faces does it have? _____

4. A hexagonal prism has 8 faces and 18 edges. How many vertices does it have? _____

5. Complete the table.

Pyramid

Edges of Base	3		
Number of Vertices			
Total Number of Edges			

Decide if each statement is true or false.

6. A hexagonal pyramid has a total of 13 edges.

   _____

7. A pyramid with 7 edges on its base has a total of 14 edges.

   _____

8. The number of edges on the base of a pyramid is twice the total number of edges.

   _____

Exploring Nets

Circle the design or designs that form a net for the
solid described.

1. cube

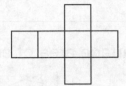 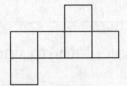

2. triangular pyramid

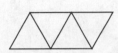

3. square pyramid

 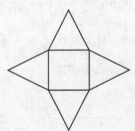

4. rectangular prism

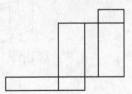 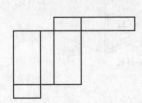

5. Design a net for a pyramid. Draw your net below.

Exploring Surface Area

1. Write the formula to find the surface area of any rectangular prism.

_____

_____

Use a calculator to find the surface area of each figure.

2.

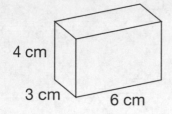

4 cm

3 cm

6 cm

_____

3.

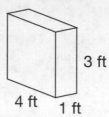

3 ft

4 ft   1 ft

_____

4.

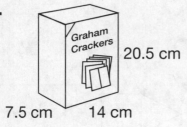

Graham
Crackers

20.5 cm

7.5 cm   14 cm

_____

5.

Baking
Soda

4 in.

2.5 in.   3.5 in.

_____

6.

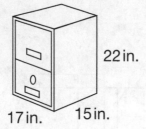

22 in.

17 in.   15 in.

_____

7.

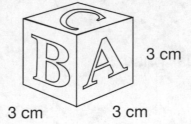

C
B A

3 cm

3 cm   3 cm

_____

8. A gallon of paint covers about 400 ft². How many gallons would you need to paint the walls of a room 10 ft wide, 14 ft long, and 8 ft tall?

_____

9. Suppose you have a 3 ft by 3 ft by 4 ft toy box with a lid. You want to paint the inside and outside of the box. What is the total surface area that you have to paint?

_____

Decision Making

You want to build several bookcases.

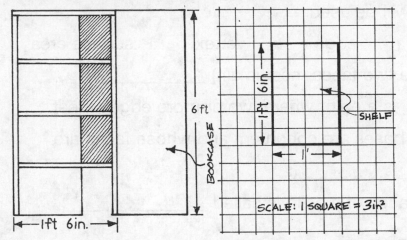

1 ft by 12 ft boards cost $16. Each additional foot costs
$1.75. You have $40 to spend on wood.

1. Into what geometric figures will the board be cut? _____

2. How much wood can you afford?

_____

3. What length of wood will you need for:

    a. the 2 sides? _____

    b. the 3 shelves? _____

    c. the top? _____

4. How many bookcases can you
make with the wood you can afford? _____

5. Can you make another bookcase with the leftover wood? _____

6. Should you buy any boards less than 12 ft long?
Explain your reasoning.

_____

_____

_____

7. How much more money would
you need to make another bookcase? _____

Name _____

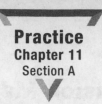
Review and Practice

Vocabulary Use a word from the list to complete each sentence. Not all words will be used.

| pyramid | prism | edge | vertex | surface area |

1. A line segment where two faces meet is a(n) _____.

2. A(n) _____ is a point where two or more edges meet.

3. A solid figure whose bases are congruent and whose faces are rectangles is a(n) _____.

4. The total area of all faces of a solid is called _____.

(Lessons 1 and 2) Complete.

5. The base of a pentagonal prism has _____ sides.

6. A solid with rectangular faces and a triangular base is a _____ prism.

7. A heptagonal prism has _____ faces.

(Lesson 3) Name the solid each net makes.

8.

9.

10.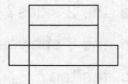

_____   _____   _____

(Lesson 4) Find the surface area of each figure.

11.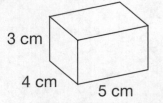

3 cm
4 cm
5 cm

12.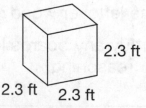

2.3 ft
2.3 ft
2.3 ft

_____   _____

(Mixed Review) Write the simplest form for each fraction.

13. $\frac{21}{35}$ = _____

14. $\frac{33}{36}$ = _____

Ounces, Pounds, and Tons

Complete. Check the reasonableness of your answer.

1. 4 lb = _____ oz

2. 1 T = _____ lb

3. 6,000 lb = _____ T

4. 32 oz = _____ lb

5. 112 oz = _____ lb

6. 5 T = _____ lb

7. 5 lb 3 oz = _____ oz

8. 40 oz = _____ lb _____ oz

9. 3 T 21 lb = _____ lb

10. 100 oz = _____ lb _____ oz

11. 20,000 lb = _____ T

12. 4 T 100 lb = _____ lb

13. 9 lb 5 oz = _____ oz

14. 2,340 lb = _____ T _____ lb

15. 7 T 15 lb = _____ lb

16. 82 oz = _____ lb _____ oz

17. Which is less, 2 T or 2,600 lb? Explain.

_____

18. Which is less, 50 ounces or 4 lb? Explain.

_____

19. Which is greater, 3 T or 5,999 lb? Explain.

_____

20. Which is greater, 5 lb 9 ounces or 90 ounces? Explain.

_____

21. Estimate the number of pounds in 700 ounces. _____

22. Estimate the number of tons in 19,680 pounds. _____

Grams and Kilograms

Use mental math to change to kilograms or grams.

1. 3 kg = _____ g   **2.** 2,500 g = _____ kg

3. 6.8 kg = _____ g   **4.** 4,301 g = _____ kg

5. 0.022 kg = _____ g   **6.** 1.542 kg = _____ g

7. 35,000 g = _____ kg   **8.** 89,901 g = _____ kg

9. 77 g = _____ kg   **10.** 100 kg = _____ g

11. 2.21 kg = _____ g   **12.** 2 g = _____ kg

13. 978 g = _____ kg   **14.** 6,082 g = _____ kg

15. 0.23 kg = _____ g   **16.** 20.4 kg = _____ g

17. How many kilograms?   **18.** How many grams?

Yogurt 227 g   15 kg

_____   _____

19. How many kilograms?   **20.** How many grams?

   Lip Balm 4.5 g    FLOUR 12.35 kg

_____   _____

21. Apples cost $2.20 per kilogram. You need 500 g of apples to put in a fruit salad. How much money will you need to buy the apples?

_____

Temperature

Write each temperature in Celsius and Fahrenheit.

1.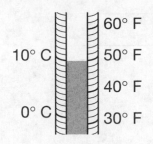

_____

2.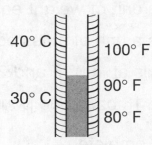

_____

3.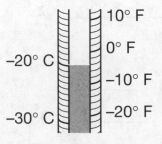

_____

4.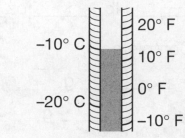

_____

5.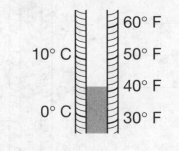

_____

6.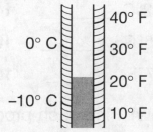

_____

Find each change in temperature.

7. 22°C to 36°C _____

8. 18°F to 32°F _____

9. 40°F to 12°F _____

10. –2°C to –30°C _____

11. –5°C to 14°C _____

12. 86°F to 101°F _____

13. Which decrease in temperature would feel cooler: 35°C
or 35°F? Explain.

_____

_____

Name _____

Review and Practice

Vocabulary Write true or false for each statement.

1. A ton is a unit of weight equal to 2,000 lb. _____

2. A gram is a unit of mass equal to 1,000 kg. _____

3. Water boils at 100° F and 212°C. _____

4. There are 16 oz in one pound. _____

(Lesson 6) Complete.

5. 80 oz = _____ lb   6. 8 T = _____ lb

7. 54 oz = _____ lb _____ oz   8. 31 lb = _____ oz

(Lesson 7) Complete.

9. 1.45 kg = _____ g   10. 34,980 g = _____ kg

11. 0.0008 kg = _____ g   12. 204 g = _____ kg

(Lesson 8) Use the thermometer to find each change in temperature.

13. 35°C to 42°C _____   14. 32°F to –4°F _____

15. –7°C to 15°C _____   16. 50°F to 83°F _____

17. 18°F to 37°F _____   18. 28°C to –1°C _____

(Mixed Review) Find each product or quotient.

19.   8 1 9
    ×   2 6

20.   2 7 1
    ×   3 8

21.   3 5 8
    ×   4 6

22. 16)‾58   23. 12)‾37   24. 15)‾72

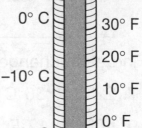
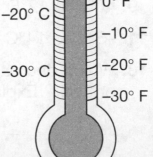

Exploring Volume

Find each volume.

1.

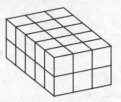

_____ units^3

2.

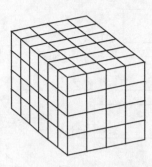

_____ units^3

3.

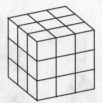

_____ units^3

4.

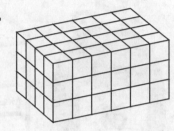

_____ units^3

Complete.

4. l = 10 cm

w = 5 cm

h = 5 cm

V = [   ]

5. l = 8 in.

w = 3 in.

h = 5 in.

V = [   ]

6. l = 10 ft

w = 10 ft

h = 8.5 ft

V = [   ]

7. l = 6 ft

w = 8 ft

h = 11 ft

V = [   ]

8. Use mental math to estimate the volume of
a box whose dimensions are 11 m × 17 m × 13 m. _____

Customary Units of Capacity

Complete.

1. 1 pt = ☐ qt

2. 2 qt = ☐ c

3. $\frac{1}{2}$ gal = ☐ fl oz

4. $\frac{1}{2}$ c = ☐ tbsp

5. 24 fl oz = ☐ pt

6. 20 pt = ☐ gal

Use the drawings to answer **7–12**.

Mayonnaise 48 fl oz   Apple Cider 1$\frac{1}{2}$ gal   MILK MILK $\frac{1}{2}$ gal   Maple syrup 1 pt 12 fl oz   Vinegar 1 pt   Barbecue sauce 28 fl oz

7. ☐ pt of mayonnaise

8. ☐ qt of apple cider

9. ☐ c of milk

10. ☐ c of maple syrup

11. ☐ oz of vinegar

12. ☐ pt of barbecue sauce

13. Nathan says 2 gallons is greater than 200 fl oz. Is he correct? Explain.

_____

_____

Metric Units of Capacity

Complete.

1. 8,000 mL = [ ] L

2. 750 mL = [ ] L

3. 3 L = [ ] mL

4. 3.75 L = [ ] mL

5. 36 mL = [ ] L

6. 4 L = [ ] mL

7. 40 L = [ ] mL

8. 400 L = [ ] mL

9. 0.4 L = [ ] mL

10. 1.75 L = [ ] mL

11. 480 mL = [ ] L

12. 50 mL = [ ] L

13. 0.22 L = [ ] mL

14. 0.059 L = [ ] mL

15. 16 mL = [ ] L

16. 1 mL = [ ] L

17. 0.71 L = [ ] mL

18. 1.6 L = [ ] mL

19. 4,360 mL = [ ] L

20. 621 mL = [ ] L

Use the drawings to answer **21–24**.

75 mL
Vanilla

MILK
3.5 L

50 mL
Perfume

JUICE
0.25 L

21. [ ] mL of milk

22. [ ] mL of juice

23. [ ] L of perfume

24. [ ] L of vanilla

Connecting Volume, Mass, and Capacity

Write the number for each.

1. 1,800 mL of water would fill a(n) ☐ cm³ container.

2. 2.9 kg of water would fill a(n) ☐ mL container.

3. 1.25 L water has a mass of ☐ kg.

4. A 50 cm³ container can hold ☐ L.

5. Complete.

A. 45 × 20 × 20 cm³   **B.** 25 × 22 × 26 cm³   **C.** 15 × 12 × 10 cm³   **D.** Mass of water = 20.5 kg

	Volume (cm³)	Amount of Water (L)	Amount of Water (mL)	Mass of Water (kg)	Mass of Water (g)
Aquarium A					
Aquarium B					
Aquarium C					
Aquarium D					

6. Describe how you can calculate the amount and mass of water an aquarium can hold if you know its dimensions.

_____

Compare Strategies: Solve a Simpler Problem/Draw a Picture

Use Solve a Simpler Problem to solve the problem.

1. Mr. Mansfield likes to make pancakes for visitors. His basic recipe makes enough for 2 adults and 1 child. The recipe calls for 2 cups of flour and 2 eggs. Mr. Mansfield wants to know how much flour he needs to make pancakes for 10 adults and 5 children.

   a. How much flour will he need to make pancakes for 4 adults and 2 children? _____

   b. How much flour will he need to make pancakes for 6 adults and 3 children? _____

   c. How many people could he serve if he used 8 cups of flour? _____

   d. How much flour will he need to make pancakes for 10 adults and 5 children? _____

   e. Describe the pattern you see.

   _____

   _____

   _____

Use Solve a Simpler Problem or any strategy to solve each problem.

2. Regina plants her tomato garden in rows of 6 and labels her plants with letters of the alphabet. For example, the plants in the first row were labeled A–F. In which row is plant W located?

   _____

3. Mrs. Maynor has an interesting doll collection. Half of her dolls are baby dolls and $\frac{2}{3}$ of these are antique. The other half are fashion and rag dolls. All 15 of her fashion dolls are quite new but they only make up $\frac{1}{10}$ of the collection. How many antique baby dolls does she have?

   _____

Name _____

Review and Practice

Vocabulary Write a definition for each word.

1. mass _____

_____

2. volume _____

_____

(Lesson 9) Find each volume.

3.

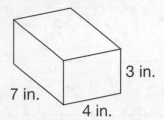

7 in. 4 in. 3 in.

_____

4.

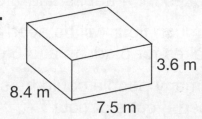

8.4 m 7.5 m 3.6 m

_____

(Lessons 10 and 11) Complete.

5. 64 fl oz = _____ c

6. $6\frac{1}{2}$ gal = _____ pt

7. 10 tbsp = _____ fl oz

8. 48 fl oz = _____ qt

9. 0.5 L = _____ mL

10. 893 mL = _____ L

(Lesson 12) Complete.

11.

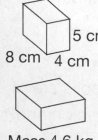

8 cm 4 cm 5 cm

Mass 4.6 kg

Volume (cm³)	Amount of Liquid (L)	Amount of Liquid (mL)	Mass of Liquid (kg)	Mass of Liquid (g)

(Mixed Review) Find each product.

12. $\frac{6}{9} \times \frac{5}{6} =$ _____

13. $\frac{8}{10} \times \frac{3}{4} =$ _____

Cumulative Review

(Chapter 1 Lesson 4) Find the range, mode, and median for each set of data.

1. 6, 16, 21, 6, 17

range _____

mode _____

median _____

2. 1.5, 10, 9.8, 6.2, 5.7, 3, 4.5

range _____

mode _____

median _____

(Chapter 2 Lesson 18) Find each difference.

3. $6.2 0
   − 2.4 9

4. $3 4.0 0
   − 5.7 5

5. $4.0 2
   − 0.5 3

6.   3.4 1
   − 1.8 8

(Chapter 9 Lesson 3) Use rounding, benchmarks, or compatible numbers to estimate each product.

7. $\frac{3}{4} \times 81$ _____

8. $3\frac{2}{7} \times 10$ _____

9. $1\frac{2}{3} \times 8$ _____

10. $\frac{5}{9} \times 22$ _____

(Chapter 10 Lessons 11 and 13) Find each area.

11.   8 cm
   24 cm

12.   1.4 mm
   2.3 mm

13.   18 ft
   5 ft

_____   _____   _____

(Chapter 11 Lesson 7) Complete.

14. 385 kg = _____ g

15. 68 g = _____ kg

16. 19.3 kg = _____ g

17. 6,472 g = _____ kg

(Chapter 11 Lesson 8) Find each change in temperature.

18. 27°C to 8°C _____

19. 18°F to −7°F _____

20. −5°C to 19°C _____

21. 82°F to 45°F _____

Name _____

Ratios

Write each ratio in three ways. Simplify.

1. cats to kittens _____ _____ _____

2. puppies to dogs _____ _____ _____

3. rabbits to bunnies _____ _____ _____

4. chicks to chickens _____ _____ _____

5. large fish to small fish _____ _____ _____

6. ducklings to ducks _____ _____ _____

7. Which shows the ratio 1:2? _____ 1:3? _____

A. frogs to tadpoles　　**B.** tadpoles to frogs　　**C.** frogs to tadpoles

Patterns in Ratio Tables

Complete.

1.

7	14			35
8		24		40

2.

3	6		12	
5			20	25

3.

5	10	15		
	12		24	30

4.

	8	12		20
10		30	40	

5.

	4		8	10
9	18	27		

6.

7		21	28	
		33		55

7. In a game, each player gets 3 letter cubes. Complete the ratio table that shows how many letter cubes for 2, 3, 4, 5, or 6 players.

Number of Players		3		5	6
Number of Cubes	6				

8. A table of equal ratios includes $\frac{10}{35}$.

    a. Name another ratio in the table. _____

    b. Write a proportion for these ratios.

_____

9. A table of equal ratios includes $\frac{12}{18}$.

    a. Name another ratio in the table. _____

    b. Write a proportion for these ratios.

_____

Exploring Equal Ratios

Complete.

1. This graph shows two ordered pairs of equal ratios. Name the ratio it shows.

_____

2. Plot another ratio on the graph that is equal to the others. Name the ratio.

_____

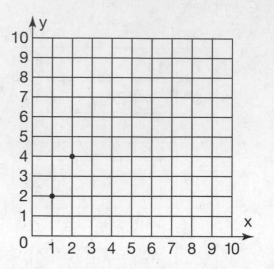

Use grid paper. Plot the ordered pairs from each ratio table on the graph.

3.

4	8	12	16	20
3	6	9	12	15

4.

1	2	3	4	5
3	6	9	12	15

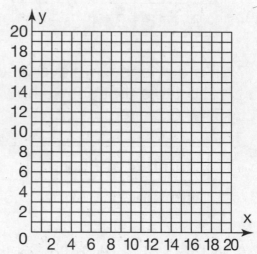

Plot a set of equal ratios on each graph.

5.

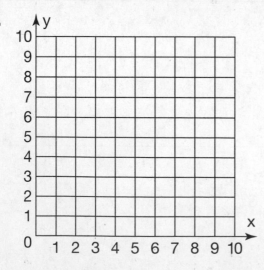

6.

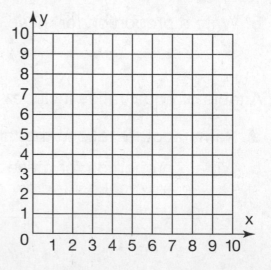

Decision Making

Solve each problem.

1. A scale drawing of a car used the ratio
   of 1 in. to 12 in. In the drawing, the diameter
   of the front wheel measured 2 in. What
   was the diameter of the wheel on the car? _____

2. The scale used by a map-maker was 1 cm
   to 15 km. If the distance between 2 cities
   is 60 km, how far apart will they be on the map? _____

3. The Empire State Building is 1,250 ft tall. A toy model
   is built to a scale of 1 in. to 50 ft. How tall is the model?

   _____

4. A scale drawing of a garden is 4 in. by 5 in. The real garden
   is 20 ft by 25 ft. What does 1 in. represent in the drawing?

   _____

5. David is making a scale model of the moon, and he
   wants to use a beach ball. The diameter of the moon is
   2,160 mi. The diameter of the beach ball is 3 ft.

   a. On David's model, how many
      miles could be represented by 1 ft? _____

   b. How many miles could be represented by 1 in.?

   _____

6. A picture of a whale uses the scale 1 cm to 3 m. If
   the whale is actually 12 m long, how long is it in the drawing?

   _____

7. A billboard artist drew a glass of milk 18 ft tall. The real
   glass of milk she copied was 6 in. tall.

   a. At the same scale, how tall will she
      have to draw an apple that is 3 in. tall? _____

   b. How long should she draw a banana that is 8 in. long?

   _____

Name _____

Review and Practice

Vocabulary Complete each sentence with a word from the list.

proportion   scale   equal ratios

1. A _____ is a statement that two ratios are equal.

2. Ratios that give the same comparison are called _____ .

3. A _____ is a ratio that shows the relationship between a scale drawing and the actual object.

(Lesson 1) Write each ratio in three ways. Simplify.

4. pencils to erasers

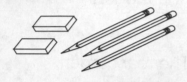

_____ _____

_____

5. rectangles to triangles

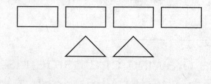

_____ _____

_____

(Lesson 2) Complete.

6. For an essay test, the teacher gave 4 sheets of paper to each student. Complete a ratio table to show how many sheets would be given out in all if there were 1, 2, 3, 4, or 5 students needing paper.

Students	1				
Paper	4				

(Lesson 3) Plot the ordered pairs from the ratio table on the graph.

7.

3	6	9	12
1	2	3	4

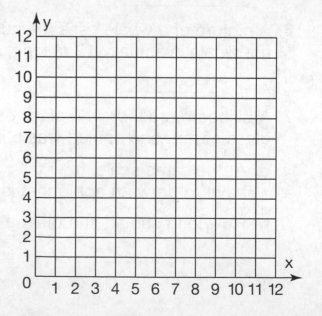

(Mixed Review) Write two equivalent fractions for each fraction.

8. $\frac{3}{10}$ = _____ = _____

9. $\frac{16}{20}$ = _____ = _____

Name _____

Exploring Percent Patterns

1. Use the table to help you complete these sentences.

Halves	Fifths	Tenths	Percents
		$\frac{1}{10}$	10%
	$\frac{1}{5}$	$\frac{2}{10}$	20%
		$\frac{3}{10}$	30%
	$\frac{2}{5}$	$\frac{4}{10}$	40%
$\frac{1}{2}$		$\frac{5}{10}$	50%

   a. Equivalents of tenths are multiples of _____ %.

   b. Equivalents of fifths are multiples of _____ %.

   c. Equivalents of halves are multiples of _____ %.

Complete each pattern. You may use a calculator to help.

2. $\frac{1}{8}$ = _____ %

$\frac{2}{8}$ = _____ %

$\frac{3}{8}$ = _____ %

$\frac{4}{8}$ = _____ %

3. $\frac{1}{4}$ = _____ %

$\frac{2}{4}$ = _____ %

$\frac{3}{4}$ = _____ %

$\frac{4}{4}$ = _____ %

4. $\frac{1}{6}$ = _____ %

$\frac{2}{6}$ = _____ %

$\frac{3}{6}$ = _____ %

$\frac{4}{6}$ = _____ %

5. $\frac{1}{3}$ = _____ %

$\frac{2}{3}$ = _____ %

$\frac{3}{3}$ = _____ %

6. Explain how knowing $\frac{1}{2}$ = 50% can help you to find the percent equivalent of $\frac{2}{4}$.

_____

Estimating Percent of a Number

Estimate.

1. 76% of 80 _____

2. 61% of 20 _____

3. 30% of 32 _____

4. $16\frac{2}{3}$% of 54 _____

5. 22% of 40 _____

6. 49% of 200 _____

7. 64% of 60 _____

8. 12.5% of 41 _____

9. 27% of 99 _____

10. 19% of 40 _____

11. 75% of 82 _____

12. 71% of 110 _____

13. 42% of 105 _____

14. 12.5% of 161 _____

15. 67% of 20 _____

16. 32% of 152 _____

16. Explain how finding 25% of 160 can help you estimate 73% of 160.

_____

_____

17. Explain how finding $\frac{1}{6}$ of 18 can help you find $16\frac{2}{3}$% of 17.

_____

_____

18. Amanda says she can use the benchmark $\frac{1}{4}$ to estimate the sale price of a hat that is 75% off. Explain how she can do this.

_____

_____

Finding Percent of a Number

Choose a method. Find the percent of each.

1. 4% of 7.25 = _____

2. 10% of 8 = _____

3. 80% of $8.20 = _____

4. 45% of 800 = _____

5. 25% of 500 = _____

6. 85% of 40 = _____

7. 75% of 24 = _____

8. 30% of $89 = _____

9. 8% of 64 = _____

10. 12% of 450 = _____

11. 65% of 720 = _____

12. 50% of 126 = _____

13. 5% of 800 = _____

14. 15% of 200 = _____

15. 23% of 400 = _____

16. 6% of 10 = _____

17. 95% of 575 = _____

18. 53% of 120 = _____

19. 48% of 82 = _____

20. 25% of 280 = _____

21. 80% of 650 = _____

22. 30% of 400 = _____

23. Since 30% of 60 = 18, 60% of 60 = _____

Explain. _____

24. Since 80% of 45 = 36, 40% of 90 = _____

Explain. _____

_____

25. If a percent of a number equals the
number, what percent of the number was taken? _____

Name _____

Review and Practice

Vocabulary

1. Give 5 examples of common percent benchmarks.

_____

(Lesson 5) Complete each pattern. You may use a calculator to help.

2. $\frac{6}{25} =$ _____ %   **3.** $\frac{9}{20} =$ _____ %

$\frac{7}{25} =$ _____ % $\frac{10}{20} =$ _____ %

$\frac{8}{25} =$ _____ % $\frac{11}{20} =$ _____ %

$\frac{9}{25} =$ _____ % $\frac{12}{20} =$ _____ %

(Lesson 6) Estimate.

4. $33\frac{1}{3}$% of 70 _____   **5.** 18% of 51 _____

6. 11% of 99 _____   **7.** 25% of 844 _____

(Lesson 7) Find the percent of each.

8. 3% of 4.5 = _____   **9.** 12% of 14 = _____

10. 48% of $50,000 = _____   **11.** 1% of $3.45 = _____

12. 90% of 83 = _____   **13.** 7% of 24.8 = _____

14. 15% of $25.15 = _____   **15.** 100% of 21 = _____

16. 42% of 103 = _____   **17.** 99% of 23 = _____

(Mixed Review) Multiply or divide.

18. $\begin{array}{r} 256 \\ \times\ \ 3.41 \end{array}$ **19.** $\begin{array}{r} 509 \\ \times\ \ 4.87 \end{array}$ **20.** $\begin{array}{r} 360 \\ \times\ \ 13.9 \end{array}$

21. $35\overline{)469}$ **22.** $83\overline{)8,597}$ **23.** $21\overline{)\$2.31}$

Exploring Fairness

Complete the table. Tell if the probability of the outcomes is
equally likely or not. If the outcomes are not equal, tell which
outcome is more likely. Then decide if the situation is fair or unfair.

	Situation	Probability of Outcome	Fairness
1.	Spin the spinner. Outcomes: 1, 3, 5, or 7		
2.	Choose a coin. Outcomes: dime, quarter, or nickel		
3.	Draw a card. Outcomes: A or B		
4.	Draw a card. Outcomes: odd or even		

5. What are the possible outcomes of two spins of the spinner in **1**?

_____

_____

6. Two cubes are painted red on 3 sides and blue on 3 sides. Tina and
Charlene toss the cubes. Tina earns one point when both cubes land
with one color up. Charlene earns one point if the cubes land with
both colors up. Is this a fair game? Explain.

_____

_____

7. Sam and Randy have a bag of marbles. There are 20 red marbles and
25 blue marbles. In turn, they reach into the bag without looking and
take out 2 marbles. Sam earns one point if both marbles are the same
color. Randy earns one point if the marbles are different colors. Is this
a fair game? Explain.

_____

Exploring Predicting from Samples

A bowl contains black beans, red beans, and white beans.
The list shows the results of three samples.

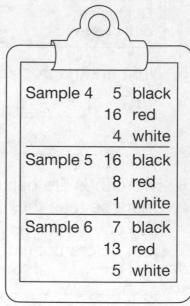

1. a. How many beans are there
all together in the 3 samples? _____

   b. How many black
   beans were in the samples? _____

   c. How many red beans were in the

   samples? _____

   d. How many white beans were in the

   samples? _____

Sample 1	11	black
	10	red
	4	white
Sample 2	8	black
	12	red
	5	white
Sample 3	15	black
	10	red

2. Predict the most
common color bean. _____

3. Predict the least
common color bean. _____

4. If sample 2 were the only sample,
what color bean would you
predict to be the most common? _____

Three more samples (4, 5, 6) were taken.

5. In samples 4–6:

   a. What was the most
   common color bean? _____

   b. What was the least
   common color bean? _____

Sample 4	5	black
	16	red
	4	white
Sample 5	16	black
	8	red
	1	white
Sample 6	7	black
	13	red
	5	white

6. In samples 1–6 how many beans were:

   a. black   **b.** white   **c.** red

   _____   _____   _____

7. Describe the number of each color bean you think is in the bowl.

_____

_____

Exploring Predicting from Experiments

Write the numbers 1, 3, 5, 7, and 9 twice, each on separate slips of paper. Put the slips of paper in a bag and use them to answer **1–7**.

1. Experiment to find how many different sums will occur by selecting 2 slips of paper. _____

2. Which do you think is more likely to occur; a sum of 10 or a sum of 4? Explain.

   _____

   _____

3. Is the chance of getting an odd number sum certain, likely, equally likely as unlikely, or impossible? Explain.

   _____

4. Which 4 sums are least likely to occur? _____

5. Name one sum that will never occur.

   _____

6. What do you think is more likely to occur when you take 2 slips of paper: getting 2 different numbers or 2 matching numbers? Explain.

   _____

   _____

7. Which do you think is more likely to occur; getting a sum less than 10 or a sum greater than or equal to 10? Explain.

   _____

   _____

Analyzing Strategies:
Make an Organized List

1. James won 4 trophies for sports. He won 1 each for
soccer, football, basketball, and tennis. How many
different ways can he arrange his trophies in a straight
line on his bedroom shelf?

    a. Call the sports S, F, B, and T. List all the combinations
    if S is the first trophy on the shelf.

    _____

    b. If F is first: _____

    c. If B is first: _____

    d. If T is first: _____

    e. How many different ways
    can the trophies be arranged? _____

2. The next year, James wins another trophy for hockey.
How many different ways can he arrange the 5 trophies?

_____

3. The football team will choose 2 colors for their uniforms.
They can choose white, red, blue, or gold. A red and
white uniform is the same as a white and red uniform.
How many color combinations can they choose?

_____

4. The basketball team travels 26 miles from school to their
game. They have been traveling for 20 minutes. When
they travel 5 miles farther, they will be halfway there.
How far have they traveled?

_____

Expressing Probabilities as Fractions

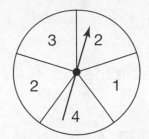 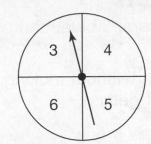

A quiz show contestant spins each spinner once and adds the numbers together. If the sum is 6 or 8, the contestant wins $100. If the sum is 4 or 10, the contestant wins $1,000.

Make tree diagrams to show the possible sums. Give the probability of each sum as a fraction. Simplify.

1. 7 _____ **2.** 4 _____ **3.** 5 _____

4. 6 _____ **5.** 8 _____ **6.** 9 _____

7. 10 _____ **8.** 6 or 8 _____ **9.** 4 or 10 _____

10. What is the probability of getting a sum of 2? _____

11. What is the probability of gettting
a sum of 4, 5, 6, 7, 8, 9, or 10? _____

12. Does the contestant have a greater
chance of winning $100 or $1,000? _____

13. There are 3 red, 5 green, and 4 yellow marbles in a bag.
Without looking, you choose one. Give the probability of
choosing a marble of each color. Express as a fraction.
Simplify.

a. red _____ **b.** green _____ **c.** yellow _____

Exploring Expected and Experimental Results

A bag contains 5 red markers, 3 blue markers, and 2 green markers.

1. If you select one marker without looking, what is the expected probability of getting:

    a. a red marker? _____   **b.** a blue marker? _____

    c. a green marker? _____   **d.** a purple marker? _____

2. Suppose you select a marker, record its color, and put it back in the bag. If you repeat this 50 times, how many times would you expect to select:

    a. a red marker? _____   **b.** a blue marker? _____

    c. a green marker? _____   **d.** a pink marker? _____

Use the spinner to answer **3–6**. Decide whether each result is likely or unlikely.

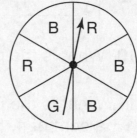

3. Outcome: R

    Trial: 36 spins

    Result: Get R, 14 times

    _____

4. Outcome: B

    Trial: 300 spins

    Result: Get B, 98 times

    _____

5. Outcome: G

    Trial: 120 spins

    Result: Get G, 95 times

    _____

6. Outcome: R or G

    Trial: 200 spins

    Result: Get R or G 95 times

    _____

7. A 1–6 number cube is tossed 200 times. About how many times would a number greater than 3 be expected?

    _____

Review and Practice

Vocabulary Write a definition for each.

1. outcome _____

2. probability _____

_____

(Lesson 8) Use the spinner to answer **3** and **4**.
Write if each game is fair or unfair.

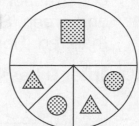

3. Player 1 gets 1 point if the spinner lands
on a square. Player 2 gets 1 point if
the spinner lands on a circle or a triangle. _____

4. Player 1 gets 1 point if the spinner lands on a square.
Player 2 gets 1 point if the spinner lands on a triangle. _____

(Lesson 9) A bag contains different numbers of the letters
A, B, C, and D. Use the sample results to answer **5** and **6**.

Sample 1   Sample 2   Sample 3

5. Predict the most common letter in the bag. _____

6. If Sample 1 were the only sample, what
would you predict for the most common letter? _____

(Lessons 10, 11, and 13) Give all the outcomes for the
experiment. Write whether they are equally likely or not.

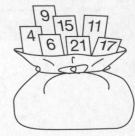

7. Choose one number from the bag.

_____

(Lesson 12) The numbers 1, 2, 7, 9, 12, and 13 are in
a bag. Give the probability of each outcome as a fraction.

8. of pulling out an even number _____

9. of pulling out an odd number _____

(Mixed Review) Find each sum or difference.

10. $4.7 + 13.19 =$ _____   **11.** $51.8 - 27.36 =$ _____

Cumulative Review

(Chapter 8 Lesson 13) Solve. Use any strategy.

1. Aaron gave half of his change to a friend. He then lost 5 cents. He had 50 cents left. How much money did he begin with? _____

2. Tamara has a total of 12 sheets of construction paper. She has only red and green. She has 4 fewer green sheets than red. How many red sheets does she have? _____

(Chapter 9 Lesson 5) Find each product. Simplify.

3. $\frac{3}{4} \times \frac{4}{5} =$ _____

4. $\frac{5}{7} \times \frac{7}{9} =$ _____

5. $\frac{5}{6} \times \frac{6}{10} =$ _____

6. $\frac{5}{8} \times \frac{3}{5} =$ _____

(Chapter 11 Lesson 4) Find the surface area of each figure.

7.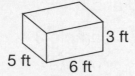
3 ft
5 ft   6 ft

8.
3.6 cm

_____   _____

(Chapter 11 Lesson 11) Complete.

9. 0.9 L = _____ mL

10. 560 mL = _____ L

(Chapter 12 Lesson 1) Write each ratio in three ways. Simplify.

11.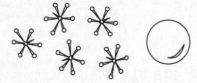

12.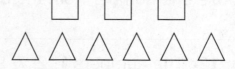

_____   _____

_____   _____

(Chapter 12 Lesson 7) Find the percent of each number.

13. 15% of $28 = _____

14. 50% of 213 = _____